**AMONG SERIOUS PROGRAMMERS**
**C IS BECOMING THE LANGUAGE OF CHOICE**

SOFTWARE SPARE PARTS: *C Language Routines and Utilities* is a library of expertly prewritten subprograms for everything from text processing to matrix algebra, from data conversion to graphics. It equips the programmer with a wide range of flexible routines that can easily be plugged into a larger program. Any one of the 140 software "spare parts" in this book can save you hours in programming time. Designed to run on any computer outfitted with a standard C compiler, this valuable collection is an indispensable resource for the professional C programmer or serious amateur.

# SOFTWARE SPARE PARTS
## C LANGUAGE ROUTINES AND UTILITIES

KENT PORTER has been a computer professional for two decades and was one of the pioneers of the microcomputer revolution. He is the author of a dozen computer-related books, including *The New American Computer Dictionary, Practical Programming in Pascal,* and *Beginning with Basic* (all available in Plume editions), and the *Porter's Programs* series, (available in Signet Special editions). In addition, he is a frequent contributor to *PC* magazine and other leading computer journals and has developed several commercial software products.

# SOFTWARE SPARE PARTS

## C LANGUAGE ROUTINES AND UTILITIES

## KENT PORTER

A PLUME BOOK

**NEW AMERICAN LIBRARY**

NEW YORK AND SCARBOROUGH, ONTARIO

Copyright © 1986 by Kent Porter

Several trademarks, trade names, and/or service marks appear in this book. The companies listed below are the owners of the trademarks, trade names, and/or service marks.

IBM is a trademark of International Business Machines.
MS-DOS is a trademark of Microsoft, Inc.
PC-DOS is a trademark of IBM.
Compaq is a trademark of Compaq Computer Corp.
Columbia is a trademark of Columbia Computer Corp.
Tandy is a trademark of the Tandy Corporation.
UNIX is a trademark of Bell Laboratories.
Whitesmiths C is a trademark of Whitesmiths, Ltd.
Mark Williams C is a trademark of Mark Williams Co.
Lattice C is a trademark of Lattice, Inc.
Framework is a trademark of Ashton-Tate.
Apple is a trademark of Apple Computer, Inc.
CP/M is a trademark of Digital Research, Inc.

 PLUME TRADEMARK REG. U.S. PAT. OFF. AND FOREIGN COUNTRIES
REGISTERED TRADEMARK—MARCA REGISTRADA
HECHO EN WESTFORD, MASS., U.S.A.

SIGNET, SIGNET CLASSIC, MENTOR, PLUME, MERIDIAN AND NAL BOOKS are published *in the United States* by New American Library, 1633 Broadway, New York, New York 10019, *in Canada* by The New American Library of Canada Limited, 81 Mack Avenue, Scarborough, Ontario M1L 1M8

**Library of Congress Cataloging-in-Publication Data**

Porter, Kent.
  Software spare parts.

  Includes index.
  1. C (Computer program language)   I. Title.
QA76.73.C15P67     1986       005.13′3       85-31005
ISBN 0-452-25840-5

First Printing, March, 1986

1  2  3  4  5  6  7  8  9

PRINTED IN THE UNITED STATES OF AMERICA

# CONTENTS:

## Chapter 3   Using ANSI.SYS on the IBM PC and Compatible Machines   57

### Basic group

### Enhanced group

## Chapter 4   Systems Programming Functions for the IBM PC and Compatibles   81

### BIOS Group

### DOS Group

# Chapter 5  Algebraic Functions  127

**Chapter 7   Financial Programming Functions   202**

**Chapter 8   Handy Utilities   215**

# SOFTWARE SPARE PARTS

## C LANGUAGE ROUTINES AND UTILITIES

# INTRODUCTION

*T*his book, which was written for professional programmers and serious amateurs, aims to furnish an inventory of C-language "software spare parts." The idea is to bring together, between two covers, a compendium of subprograms that you can draw upon as you develop systems. We programmers spend much of our time (sometimes too much) researching and developing processes—data conversions, machine-level operations, calculations peculiar to an application—that are unfamiliar. We spend vast amounts of time and energy "reinventing the wheel," a common euphemism among programmers. Another wail often heard is, "somebody must have done this before." This book provides a lot of those processes already written and tested so that, instead of missing deadlines because of them, you can draw them from inventory like spare parts and plug them into your programs. It's a productivity aid for C programmers.

By its nature, C lends itself to this kind of treatment. The language allows you to accumulate libraries of subprograms and then use those subprograms as though their names were actual instructions of the language. Once a subprogram (or *function,* as it's called in C) has been added to a library, your only concerns as the programmer are to furnish it with the proper data and utilize its results appropriately. This book provides you with rich opportunities to grow and tailor the C language to suit your particular requirements.

1

Most of the functions in this book are immediately usable by any C programmer, no matter what machine or operating system or brand of compiler you have. C is a highly portable language, meaning that it applies to a broad range of computers from small micros to the largest mainframes. As long as you have a C compiler that conforms to the published standards for the language, you'll have no difficulty using the great majority of "software spare parts" in this book.

At the same time, there are a fair number of these spare parts that pertain specifically to the IBM PC family of computers and to the "clones," machines that closely emulate the IBM PC, such as the Compaq, Columbia, Tandy 1x00, among many others. I have no particular IBM bias; in fact, the computer that this book was written on is a compatible, not an IBM brand. On the other hand, there is a vast community of serious computer users "out there" who abide by IBM's de facto standard, and it is the machine of preference for most of the hurricane of activity in the software development business as well as in "roll your own" programming. One might equally make a case for doing a book around the Apple systems. The trouble with that is that there are two distinct Apple technologies—the II family and the Lisa/MacIntosh group—and they haven't a blasted thing in common. Another case could be made for basing the book on CP/M. Now, as it happens, I was one of the first CP/M users, and I still have a CP/M machine that I like a lot. But again, we run into the problem of fragmented technologies. The great weakness of CP/M is that it's too general. There is no consistent means of controlling the screen, among other hardware issues. But both Apple users and CP/M users, as well as those of other wholly different environments, will find much of value in this book. I simply chose the IBM-and-clones model as being the most prevalent, and for that reason I have included some sections that are specifically targeted to the users of those machines.

One thing this book is decidedly *not* is a tutorial on how to program in C. Because the book is long and intended for serious C programmers, I have opted not to include descriptions of algorithms and detailed explanations of how the functions work. If you're a "pro" or "near-pro," you can see for yourself; if you're a novice, you need to get one of the many good introductory texts on C. My recommendations in that regard are, in order, *C Programming Guide* by Jack Purdum (Indianapolis, Ind.: Que Corporation, 1983) and, having mastered that, *The C Programming Language* by Brian W. Kernighan and Dennis M. Ritchie (Englewood Cliffs, N.J.: Prentice-Hall, Inc., 1978). The latter—usually referred to as "K&R"—is the definitive work on C, but it assumes more programming experience than Purdum's. Both these works have been invaluable aids in preparing this book, and are essential components of any C programmer's library. No doubt there are others just as good.

In developing this book, I used the DeSmet C compiler for the IBM PC. I also used the SuperSoft C compiler for CP/M systems in some sections, but SuperSoft's is not a K&R-standard product and thus does not apply to functions and operations involving floating-point values unless you use their library calls. The DeSmet product does comply with C standards, and the price is reasonable. This is not to "plug" the DeSmet product and denigrate SuperSoft. Both are good, but DeSmet is standard and SuperSoft is not. I should also note, for the sake of objective journalism, that I had to buy the DeSmet compiler and SuperSoft gave me an evaluation copy of theirs. Having read this, they probably won't be so forthcoming in the future, yet I firmly believe that it's better to stick with C compilers that adhere to standards, and this is particularly important if you write software that you expect to port to other systems.

In that same vein, it's also appropriate to say that, whereas I'm certain the functions provided here work with a K&R standard compiler, there is no way that I, or anyone else, can provide an ironclad guarantee that they'll work with your particular compiler. There are pernicious little differences that creep into diverse products developed at different times by different people, no matter how hard they try to stick to a published standard. I will guarantee that every single function and program in this book has been compiled as shown with a standard compiler and tested by more than one person. On the other hand, the oldest adage in the computer business is that "software always has bugs," and it's possible that a few have slipped past me and a host of auditors and editors and the like. Should you encounter problems with the material furnished between these covers, I recommend that you first check for typos that you might have made, and then—if pain persists—look over the section of your product's manual covering deviations from standard C. These two simple and (for the battle-scarred initiates) obvious precautions will probably solve 98 percent of the problems you might have with the materials in this book.

C is a peculiar programming language. There's nothing else quite like it, as to both its almost universal applicability and its look. It has exactly the appearance that the uninitiated think computer languages have, and in that—by some perverse quirk—it's somewhat unique. C is full of strange symbols and unblushing gobbledygook. More than one programmer has dismissed it as a "dirty" language, referring to its utter disregard for neatness and legibility. Perhaps the only other widespread language as esoteric as C is APL, also littered with weird notation, but very different in its approach and purposes. Because C is hard to read, even those of us who work with the language daily have an awful time puzzling out what an old piece of code, or one written by someone else, does. Were C not as good as it is, it probably wouldn't be worth all the trouble.

But C *is* good. Every language has some drawback. In C, it's readability. For "quick and dirty" programming—throwing something together to get a result without a lot of planning—nobody has yet come up with anything better than BASIC. The problems with BASIC are that it runs slowly, it encourages sloppy programming, and the language itself applies only to applications; ever hear of serious systems software written in BASIC? Pascal is supposed to correct the deficiencies of BASIC, and to an extent it does. On the other hand, it imposes a lot of arbitrary constraints on the programmer without delivering much more by way of real capability. Then there's COBOL, unwieldy and dreadfully verbose, an old habit the corporate world seems unable to break. COBOL is also lousy at math beyond grade-school arithmetic and at everything else except repetitive processing of masses of data and report generation. Assembler is terrific for systems work, but impossible for mathematics and infuriatingly tedious to boot. FORTRAN, nearly as hard to read as C, limits itself to the number-crunching it does so well. Ada is even more cumbersome than COBOL, Modula-2 merely a souped-up rework of Pascal, and so on. This doesn't mean these languages are bad, but rather that they're limited. Of all the programming languages in common use, and there are many not mentioned here, the only one that does everything is C.

C is sparse, lean, and surpassingly powerful. It has been used for writing everything from the UNIX operating system to general-ledger packages to trivial utilities. About the only area where C comes up short is in direct control over individual CPU registers, and that's easy to fix by resorting to small assembly-language routines. C is, in fact, a form of shorthand for assembler, its compiler a giant macroprocessor that expands terse notation into complex sequences of assembly language.

It is this very conciseness that makes C so hard to read. As examples, the file-open statement

```
if ( !fp = fopen ( "FILENAME.EXT", "r")) {
```

and the input statement

```
while ( str [ p++ ] = toupper ( getchar ()))
```

or perhaps worst of all, a complicated ternary on the order of

```
*++str = isspace ( ch = k [ p++ ] ) ? '∅' : ch;
```

are not intuitively obvious and take some getting used to, but they allow you to express, in compact form, complex activities that occupy many lines of code in other languages. This is not an apology for C's illegibility—its major flaw—but simply a fact. As a C programmer you have no doubt learned to find the logic in such statements, for they abound throughout the language (and to tell the truth, I think many programmers fall in love with C precisely because it is so esoteric).

The secret of C's extensibility lies in libraries, which are collections of PUBLIC subroutines. The general process is as follows:

1. You accumulate groups of generalized subprograms—perhaps one for text processing, another for algebraic functions, another for system-level access, etc.—in source form.
2. You compile each source library and designate it as an object library (the means for doing so varies from one C product to another).
3. You write programs that refer to library members (subprograms) as though those members were built-in instructions of the language.
4. As time goes on, you add other generalized functions to your libraries.

The net result of this process is that your own private rendition of the language gradually grows. Some functions within your libraries may never be referred to more than once, and that's okay because they occupy only disk space; if you ever need them again, they're there as a permanent part of the language. Other functions will become integral instructions for you, and you never need agonize over how to do thus and such again. You simply call that function and include the library it resides in during the link phase.

As to this book in particular, I recommend that you create a separate library for each chapter. There are three basic reasons for this. The first is that it creates a natural grouping of functions by their general purposes; should you decide later that life would be better if you had a text function that does X, you will immediately know which library to add it to. The second is that it holds libraries to manageable size. If you put every function in this book into one library, you would have an enormous and probably unmanageable library, and every time you linked to one of its functions, the link phase would take an eternity. The third is that the libraries, in the order presented here, are hierarchical in nature. C linkers, in general, resolve external references in reverse, using a one-pass methodology. As they process a library, they resolve each reference from the preceding level. They sort the references within the library, so that if function B refers to function A, that's accomplished for you automatically through function sorting. If function B from this library, however, refers to function R from the preceding library, function R will end up being unresolved, since the linker lacks the ability to look backward (toward the preceding levels). Consequently, to resolve all references, it's necessary to present the linker with the names of the libraries in the *reverse* order of their presentation in this book.

That sounds like a lot of double-talk, so let's take a specific example. Say you're doing some business program and you need to use the dollars function presented in Chapter 2. It happens that dollars calls the stround and rset functions, which appear in Chapter 1. Suppose you write a program called BUSINESS and you give the linker a statement such as

link business, textlib/s, frmtlib/s

or whatever it might be with your C product (the "/s" option in many linkers means "search the named library and include only those PUBLIC routines specifically referred to"). The following happens:

1. The linker finds PUBLICs called stround and rset in the first library (textlib) and figures nobody wants them (since they're referred to in the next library, which it hasn't gotten to yet).
2. The linker, as it progresses to the next library, forgets everything it ever knew about textlib.
3. Finding references to stround and rset in the second library, the linker says to itself, "I have to search additional libraries to find these subprograms."
4. The only additional library is the implied standard library, which comes with all C products. Unfortunately, the standard library does not contain stround and rset. As a result, the linker never finds these references because of step 2, and it reports unresolved references, which leads to programs that fail.

This sorry situation will not happen when you list the libraries in reverse order with a link statement such as

link business, frmtlib/s, textlib/s

since `stround` and `rset` are unresolved from the search of `frmtlib` and will thus be "caught" in the search of the subsequent libraries.

Other examples abound: some of the geometric functions (Chapter 6) refer to algebraic functions (Chapter 5), and monetary functions (Chapter 7) also utilize those from Chapter 5. Therefore it is essential to list libraries arising from the chapters in reverse order of presentation.

Note, incidentally, that I have carefully avoided circular references. There are no situations in which a function from Chapter 4 refers to one from Chapter 5, which in turn refers to one from Chapter 3, etc. This avoids crazy entanglements in which it is almost impossible to resolve all references. (As an aside, should you ever encounter a library containing a circular reference, you can usually overcome the problem by naming the library in the link list immediately after the program name and again at the end of the list.)

Throughout, I have religiously adhered to a standard format for the headnotes to each function, which is as follows:

## Function name

## ( parameters )

**Description:**   A discussion of the function, what it does, and the things you need to consider in calling it.

**Parameters:**   In order of stipulation, the parameters and their data types required by the function.

**Type of Value Returned:**   The data type of the value returned directly by the function, along with other considerations, such as the meanings of fixed return values (e.g., "∅ = unsuccessful, any other value means it completed successfully").

**Other Functions Called:**   In general, this item names other functions *presented in this book* that are called by the function under discussion, so that you can make sure you have included those functions ("prerequisites") in your growing library of subprograms. Standard-library functions are *not* named, even though many of these subprograms call the standard library.

**Remarks:**   This field appears in some headnotes and not in others. It contains "Oh, by the way . . ." information that is important to understanding the function, that ought to be taken into account, or that otherwise specifies your responsibilities as the programmer calling the function.

---

(The function listing itself is located under the bar)

---

The method you employ for accumulating libraries is, of course, up to you, and to some extent also a consequence of the C product you use. Your part is collecting the source code in a text file, which is the main topic we'll cover here; your C compiler governs the steps for turning the source code into linkable libraries, and for that you'll have to consult the product manual.

The easiest way to create source libraries from this book is to set up a group of text files, one for each chapter. My own personal preference is to select names that describe the general content of the library and also include the letters "LIB," so that when I look at the directory I can immediately spot the libraries. For example, the chapter on text processing brought about a library called "TEXTLIB.C," the one on data formatting another library "FRMTLIB.C," etc. Perhaps you have your own ideas on this subject, but if you don't, this one works for me.

You can then use a word processor or program editor or even (gasp!) the MS-DOS program EDLIN or CP/M's ED to type the functions you select, one after the other, into the source library. Any time you need to add another function, simply open the library, go to end-of-file, and start typing. This is probably the best method for you as the reader of this book.

An alternative is to put each function into its own file. You can give the file the same name as the function (they are all eight characters or less, which satisfies file-naming conventions in MS-DOS and CP/M), followed by the ".C" suffix. For example, the upshift function can go into a file entitled "UPSHIFT.C."

The problem with this approach is that it creates a whole bunch of files that lack unity. It's thus necessary to pull them together into a single file. For that you have a couple of alternatives.

The first method is to create a "LIB" file such as "TEXTLIB.C" whose only content is a list of C-language #includes. This constitutes a compilation unit, and as the compiler processes it, it goes out and finds each of the #included files and accumulates their object form in a linkable module (typically, a file with the same name as the source, but a suffix such as ".O"). This method does not, however, actually combine the source files into one file; you still have to maintain all those separate function files where the compiler can inspect them one by one.

A better approach is to create separate files for each function in a category, and then collect them all into a single large file. Because this was the method I used in writing this book, I made a program especially for that purpose (although it can be used for concatenation of any text files). Its name is COLLECT, and you'll find it in the Utilities chapter near the end of the book (Chapter 8). Creating a file for COLLECT is somewhat like the idea discussed in the last paragraph, except that you substitute the directive %insert for #include. You then process the file with COLLECT. Instead of merely compiling all the named source files, however, it actually pulls them into the resulting library file in source form. You can then erase all the individual function files and maintain (and compile) only the output of COLLECT. It's a technique well suited to subprogram development, because as you debug functions you need only recompile and test the one you're working on rather than the entire library. When the function is complete, pull it into the big source library with COLLECT, recompile the library, and move on to the next function.

You will no doubt discover that there are many subprograms in this book for which you cannot imagine any possible application in your work, and that's fine. Probably no programmer needs every function here, but every programmer needs some of them. If you don't see what good a particular function is, skip it.

On the other hand, several of the functions—rset, for example, which shifts text to the right side of a field—though not the compelling sorts of things that keep people awake at night or that one can't live without, are important as prerequisites to other functions presented elsewhere. There is a "cascading" effect among some of these functions. The dollars function, for example, calls stround, which is listed in the headnotes for dollars; dollars won't work unless you have also included stround in the library, because the linker will give you an "unresolved reference" error. Looking at the headnotes for stround, you'll discover that it uses another function called pos_of. This is *cascading*: dollars calls stround which calls pos_of, and therefore both subsidiary functions must be in the linkable library for dollars to work. The headnotes, however, only tell you about the functions called directly. Fortunately, there are only a few "bedrock" functions that often turn up at the tail end of cascades, and as you use the libraries you will soon uncover them.

Now that we've discussed these "software spare parts," let's get busy and put them to work.

*Program diskette*

If you'd like to save yourself a lot of typing, you can purchase an IBM-compatible DSDD diskette containing all the functions and programs in this book arranged into libraries corresponding to the chapters. Then all you have to do is compile them with your K&R standard compiler, and you'll have immediate access to the full power of these time-saving software spare parts.

To order, make your check or money order payable to California Software. The cost is $49.95 plus $2.00 shipping and handling (California residents also add $3.00 sales tax). Visa and MasterCard are also accepted; please furnish the expiration date along with your card number. Send your order to:

Bayview Software
663 South Bernardo Ave.
Suite 157
Sunnyvale, CA 94087

Orders are shipped by Priority Mail on the Monday following the week in which they are received.

# CHAPTER **1**

# TEXT PROCESSING FUNCTIONS

*T*he functions presented in this chapter lay the groundwork for those appearing later, which often refer back here for some fundamental operations. These functions comprise a library for manipulating character data either as single bytes or in character arrays, and anyone who writes programs that do more with text than simply displaying labels and prompts will sooner or later need most or all of these functions.

The chapter also includes a general-purpose (and somewhat simpleminded) utility program for sorting text files into ascending order.

The functions given in this chapter, by name and purpose, are as follows:

| | |
|---|---|
| strlen | Number of characters in a string. |
| upshift | Shifts a string to uppercase. |
| dnshift | Shifts a string to lowercase. |
| match | Finds the position of a substring within a larger string. |
| pos_of | Returns the position of a specific character within a string. |
| reverse | Reverses the order of characters within a string. |
| compstr | Compares two strings and returns an indicator showing their relationship. |

| | |
|---|---|
| swapstr | Exchanges two strings. |
| sortstr | Sorts a list of text items into order. |

The last item in the chapter is SORT, which is not a function, but instead a complete, stand-alone program, and should not be included in your library. It utilizes many of the text functions given here, and serves not only as a useful program but also as a demonstration of the functions.

## strlen

### ( string )

*Description:*  Most C compiler products come with a standard function with the same name. This function serves the same basic purpose as this one: to determine the number of characters in a string. The version given here is an improvement on the usual strlen in that it detects an improperly terminated string (one without a null at the end, which thereby violates the convention in C). When the string is properly formatted, strlen returns its length, but when the version given here detects a string of more than 255 bytes, it returns -1 as a signal that something is wrong. Testing for -1 can save your program from going haywire.

*Parameters:*  The name of a character array, or a literal string.

*Type of Value Returned:*  An integer giving the length of the string, or -1 if the string is more than 255 bytes long.

*Other Functions Called:*  None.

*Remarks:*  If you include this function in your text library, the linker will automatically bypass the standard strlen function and substitute this version instead.

The 255-byte limit is arbitrary. Set a different limit if you wish.

```
int strlen ( string )              /* length of string */
char    string [];
{
    int         p;

        p = 0;
        while ( string [ p ] != '\0' && p < 256 )
            p++;
        if ( p > 255 )
            p = -1;
        return ( p );
}
```

## upshift

## ( string )

*Description:*   Beginning at the point in a string that you pass a parameter, upshift converts all the lowercase alphabetics a . . . z to capitals. All other characters (digits, punctuation, etc.) remain unchanged after this function is called. It, in turn, uses the standard C function toupper, which is included in virtually all C products as part of the standard library.

You can begin at a point other than the first character by passing an address parameter (using the & prefix and the subscript of the point). For example, if you have a string called sentence and you want to shift from the fifth character to the end, call this function with

upshift ( &sentence [ 4 ]);

*Parameters:*   Name of a character string when shifting is to begin at the start, or the address within the string (see Description) where shifting is to begin.

*Type of Value Returned:*   Integer indicating the number of characters processed by upshift (regardless of whether or not they were actually shifted); that is, the length of the string. The shifted result is passed back in the same array given as a parameter.

*Other Functions Called:*   strlen.

*Remarks:*   Because the strlen function presented earlier is used by upshift, a -1 result indicates that the string could not be shifted (see strlen).

```
int upshift ( string )          /* shift string to all upper-case */
char    string [];
{
    int         p, length;

        if (( length = strlen ( string )) > 0 )
            for ( p = 0; p < length; p++ )
                string [ p ] = toupper ( string [ p ] );
        return ( length );
}
```

## dnshift

## ( string )

***Description:***   This function is identical to upshift, except that it shifts all capital letters A . . . Z to lowercase, beginning at the address within the string passed as a parameter.

***Parameters:***   The name of a character array when beginning at the first character, or an offset within the array as described under upshift. You can also pass a literal string as a parameter.

***Type of Value Returned:***   An integer indicating the length of the string processed (regardless of the number of characters shifted), or -1 if the function was unable to process the string.

***Other Functions Called:***   strlen.

***Remarks:***   Same as for upshift.

```
int dnshift ( string )          /* shift string to all lower-case */
char    string [ ];
{
    int         p, length;

        if (( length = strlen ( string )) > 0 )
            for ( p = 0; p < length; p++ )
                string [ p ] = tolower ( string [ p ] );
        return ( length );
}
```

## match

## ( substring, string )

*Description:* The `match` function searches a string to determine if and where the given substring is located within it. If it finds the substring—a character sequence—within the string, it returns the offset of the first character where the match occurs. For example, if you call the function with

```
match ( "name", "My name is Kent" );
```

the function returns the value 3 ("name" begins at character position 4, which is offset 3 from the start of the string). When there is no match, as in

```
match ( "John", "My name is Kent" );
```

the `match` function returns -1 as an indicator to that effect. Usually, of course, you'll call `match` with symbolic variables rather than with literals, as shown in the examples. This function is extremely useful in parsing (examining text to see whether it contains an expected character sequence, such as a keyword).

*Parameters:*

   `substring` is the character sequence to look for.
   `string` is the text to search.

*Type of Value Returned:* An integer giving the offset of the substring within the string, or -1 if:

   1. The string does not contain the substring, or;
   2. Either the string or substring is null (has no contents), or;
   3. The substring is longer than the string.

*Other Functions Called:* `strlen`

*Remarks:* `match` is *case sensitive*, meaning that it does not ignore whether letters are in upper- or lowercase. It only finds exact matches. Consequently, the statement

```
loc = match ( "kent", "My name is Kent" );
```

returns -1 to `loc`, since "kent" and "Kent" are not identical.

```
match ( substring, string )            /* pos of substring in string */
char    substring [], string [];
{
    int      s, i, f, ls, li, p;

        p = -1;
        if (( ls = strlen ( substring )) < 1 ||
            ( li = strlen (   string   )) < 1 )
                    goto quit;
        for ( i = 0; i <= li; i++ ) {
            if ( string [ i ] == substring [ 0 ] ) {
                for ( f = i, s = 0; s < ls; f++, s++ ) {
                    if ( string [ f ] != substring [ s ] )
                            goto cont;
                }
                p = i;
                goto quit;
            }                      /* end of 'if string' */
cont:           continue;         /*   'for i' loop     */
        }
quit:    return ( p );
}
```

## pos__of

## ( character, string )

**Description:** This function is similar to match, except that it searches a string or character array for a specific individual character and returns the offset of its first occurrence.

**Parameters:**

character is the character to search for.
string is the character array to be searched.

**Type of Value Returned:** An integer indicating the offset (one less than the position) of the character's first occurrence within the string, or -1 if:

1. The character does not occur within the string;
2. The string is null (has no contents).

**Other Functions Called:** strlen.

**Remarks:** pos__of is case sensitive; that is, it will not find the uppercase equivalent of a lowercase parameter or vice versa. Thus, the following call will return -1:

loc = pos__of ( 'E', "Her name is Susan" );

because the text, though it contains two lowercase letter 'e's,' does not contain the capital 'E' specified.

This function is equivalent to strchr found in many standard libraries.

```
int pos_of ( c, in_str )              /* position of char in string */
char     c, in_str [];
{
    int          i, li, p;

        p = -1;
        if (( li = strlen ( in_str )) > 0 )
            for ( i = 0; i < li; i++ ) {
                if ( in_str [ i ] == c ) {
                    p = i;
                    break;
                }
            }
        return ( p );
}
```

## reverse

## ( string )

*Description:*  reverse inverts a character array so that, if the string reads "abcde" before being passed to the function, it will have the order "edcba" afterward. Though of limited usefulness in true text processing, reverse is occasionally needed in systems programming to flip buffers where data are read (or written) in last-to-first order. It can also cause humorous effects in games and other entertainment software.

*Parameters:*  The name of the character array to be inverted. (*Note:* You can also pass string literals, but this is a dangerous business in that it alters the copy of the program in memory.)

*Type of Value Returned:*  None (alters the array directly).

*Other Functions Called:*  strlen.

*Remarks:*  reverse operates directly on the array passed as a parameter, and does not copy its results to another array. Thus, if a copy of the original array is important later in the program, use the standard function strcpy to duplicate it for safekeeping in another array before calling reverse.

```
reverse ( string )          /* reverse order of chars in string */
char    string [];
{
    int        s, d;
    char       c;

        if (( d = strlen ( string ) - 1 ) > 0 ) {
            s = 0;
            while ( s < d ) {
                c = string [ s ];
                string [ s++ ] = string [ d ];
                string [ d-- ] = c;
            }
        }
}
```

## compstr

## ( string1, string2 )

**Description:**   This function compares two character arrays and reports which is lower in collating sequence (ASCII alphabetic order). The strings do *not* have to be of equal length. The results and their meanings are described below.

**Parameters:**   The names of two character arrays (and/or string literals, if appropriate) to be compared to determine their order.

**Type of Value Returned:**   An integer in the range Ø . . . 2, the meanings of which are:

| | |
|---|---|
| Ø | The strings are identical. |
| −1 | string1 is lower than string2. |
| 1 | string2 is lower than string1. |

**Other Functions Called:**   strlen.

**Remarks:**   When strings are of differing lengths but identical throughout the length of the shorter one (for example, JON and JONES), the shorter string is considered lower in order.

   This function is similar to strcmp found in many compilers' standard libraries.

```
int compstr ( str1, str2 )  /* compare strings for collating order */
char    str1 [], str2 [];
{
    int len1, len2, result, p;

        result = -1;
        if (( len1 = strlen ( str )) < 1 )
            goto quit;
        result = 1;
        if (( len2 = strlen ( str2 )) < 1 )
            goto quit;
        for ( p = 0; p < len1, p < len2; p++ ) {
            if ( str1 [ p ] < str2 [ p ] ) {
                result = -1;
                goto quit;
            }
            if ( str1 [ p ] > str2 [ p ] ) {
                result = 1;
                goto quit;
            }
```

```
        }
        if ( len1 == len2 )
            result = 0;
        else {
            if ( p > len1 )
                result = -1;
            else
                result = 1;
        }
quit:   return ( result );
}
```

## swapstr

## ( string1, string2 )

*Description:*   swapstr, useful chiefly in sorting and other applications that involve rearranging text into ordered lists, swaps the contents of two character arrays so that, after the function does its duty, each array has replaced the other. A weakness of C has to do with the inability of a program or function to determine the maximum size of an array. As a result, this function doesn't try; it's your responsibility to ensure that each involved array is big enough to absorb the contents of the other one. If you don't, it's conceivable that a long string swapped with a short one will overflow the smaller array and clobber adjacent data areas, causing ugly things to ensue. The easiest way to defend your program from this kind of mess is to allocate character arrays large enough for any reasonable purpose; for example, 80 bytes for names, even though you only expect 25 or so characters at most. (Always anticipate that the user might do something stupid. After all, haven't you sometimes?)

*Parameters:*   The names of two character arrays to be exchanged. The arrays do not have to be of equal length (but see Description above). In general, it's a bad idea to use string literals with this function. If you do, make sure they're padded with spaces to be of equal length, lest your self-modifying program overlay adjacent code with alphanumeric garbage and go insane.

*Type of Value Returned:*   None (directly modifies the strings).

*Other Functions Called:*   None.

*Remarks:*   The maximum string size is 255 characters. If either array has more than this number, swapstr swaps only the first 255 and then appends a null terminator.

```
swapstr ( str1, str2 )          /* exchange two strings */
char    str1 [], str2 [];
{
    char    swaparea [ 256 ];
    int     i;

        for ( i = 0; i < 256; i++ )
            swaparea [ i ] = '\0';
        i = 0;
        while ( str1 [ i ] != '\0' && i < 256 ) {
            swaparea [ i ] = str1 [ i ];
            i++;
        }
        i = 0;
        while ( str2 [ i ] != '\0' && i < 256 ) {
            str1 [ i ] = str2 [ i ];
            str1 [ ++i ] = '\0';
        }
        i = 0;
        while ( swaparea [ i ] != '\0' ) {
            str2 [ i ] = swaparea [ i ];
            str2 [ ++i ] = '\0';
        }

}
```

## sortstr

## ( list, highest, entry_length )

*Description:* This function uses a common sorting algorithm to rearrange a list of strings into an ascending collating sequence (low to high). The list must be a two-dimensional array of characters with the "lines" in rows and their individual alphanumerics in columns, as is customary in text processing. It's a fairly simpleminded function; lacking the capability of working on sort keys, it evaluates the strings from left to right until it finds an inequality to determine their relative positions. Thus, if you have several fields within each line, arrange them so that the most important sort field is to the left, the second most important next, and so on, before calling this function to rearrange them.

*Parameters:*

list is the name of the two-dimensional array of characters to be sorted.

highest is an integer indicating how many actual data items (lines) the list contains.

entry_length is an integer telling the length of each element (line) in the array; that is, how many columns you allocated for the width. (*Note:* The data contents themselves do not have to be of equal length.)

*Type of Value Returned:*   None (directly alters the list).

*Other Functions Called:*   compstr, swapstr.

*Remarks:*   Although a reasonably efficient sort technique is used by sortstr, sorting is a complex CPU-bound process that can, under some circumstances, run for a considerable time. The duration of a sort can never be predicted, since it is a function of the list length, the width of the lines, and the degree to which the original data are unordered, that is, how much work sortstr has to do to rearrange it.

```
sortstr ( list, highest, ent_len )    /* sort array of strings */
char     list [];
int      highest, ent_len;
{
    int       p1, p2, swaps, spread;

        spread = highest * ent_len;
        do {
            swaps = 0;
            p1 = -ent_len;
            while (( p1 += ent_len ) <= ( spread - ent_len )) {
                p2 = p1 + ent_len;
                do {
                    if ( compstr ( &list [ p1 ], &list [ p2 ] ) == 2 ) {
                        swapstr ( &list [ p1 ], &list [ p2 ] );
                        swaps++;
                    }
                    p2 += ent_len;
                } while ( p2 <= spread );
            }     /* end of while loop */
        } while ( swaps != 0 );
}
```

## SORTTEXT

### ( filename )

*Description:*   Although written as a demonstration of the `sortstr` function presented previously, this is a complete program that is useful "as is" for ordering text files. It expects you to specify the filename in the command line. For example, to sort a file called NAMES.LST on the B: drive, type the command

        SORTTEXT B:NAMES.LST

In the version given here, the program is able to accommodate a file of up to 100 records of 80 characters each. You can modify it to suit other requirements by changing the values of the constants LENGTH (for the number of records) and WIDTH (for the maximum record length) and recompiling. The sorted results normally appear on the display screen; if your operating system supports it, use piping to redirect output to another file or the page printer. Since the program uses `sortstr`, it assumes that the fields within the record (if any) are already arranged in descending order of importance as sort keys.

*Parameters:*   A filename on the command line.

*Type of Value Returned:*   None (complete program).

*Other Functions Called:*   `sortstr`, plus the standard library.

*Remarks:*   `sortstr` and its subsidiary functions must have already been compiled and placed into a linkable library, and the link command for this program must refer to it.

```
/*  General sort utility, reads from file, outputs to screen   */
#include <stdio.h>
#define     LENGTH      100
#define     WIDTH       80

main ( argc, argv )
int         argc;
char        *argv [];
{
    int         row, p, n, cc, file;
    char        info [ LENGTH ] [ WIDTH ], buf [ 80 ];
    unsigned    array;

        row = n = p = cc = 0;
```

```
            if ( argc == 1 ) {
                puts ( "\nInclude filename in command line\n" );
                cc = 1;
                goto eoj;
            }
            if (( file = fopen ( argv [ 1 ], "r" )) == 0 ) {
                printf ( "Unable to open file %s\n", argv [ 1 ] );
                cc = 1;
                goto eoj;
            }
            printf ( "\n--- Reading text file %s", argv [ 1 ] );
            array = &info;
            while ( fgets ( array, WIDTH, file ) != 0 ) {
                n++;
                array += WIDTH;
            }
            printf ( "\n--- Read %d records", n );
            if ( n > 0 ) {
                puts ( "\n--- Sorting\n" );
                sortstr ( info, n - 1, WIDTH );
                for ( row = 0; row <= n; row++ )
                    puts ( info [ row ] );            /* sorted results */
            }
eoj:        puts ( "\nSORT ended\n" );
            exit ( cc );
}
```

# CHAPTER **2**

# DATA FORMATTING FUNCTIONS

*T*his chapter brings together a number of assorted functions that reformat existing data. You'll find these facilities useful for creating "pretty" output, and also for converting between bit- and byte-oriented data formats. They expand upon and thus enhance the formatting controls available in the standard C functions printf and sprintf.

Because many of the functions given here involve conversions to, from, or within character arrays, they occasionally refer to other functions from the earlier chapter on text processing. For example, stround, which rounds a string of digits, draws upon the function pos_of. Obviously, for stround to work, you must already have compiled pos_of, and its name (or the name of the library that contains it) must be included in the linker command-line so that it can be included in a program that uses stround. Throughout this book, the headnotes preceding each function's listing note what other functions it uses that are not in the standard C library.

The formatting functions in this chapter are:

| | |
|---|---|
| rset | Shifts character data to the right side of a field. |
| lset | Shifts character data to the left side of a field. |
| stround | Rounds a numeric string to a specified number of decimal places. |

| | |
|---|---|
| dollars | Reformats a numeric string into monetary notation, rounding as necessary. |
| ck_wtr | Converts an amount to English words, suitable for writing bank checks. |
| atox | Converts a byte to hexadecimal notation. |
| itox | Signed integer to hex notation. |
| utox | Unsigned integer to hex notation. |
| xtoa | Hex to its corresponding byte. |
| xtoi | Hex to an integer. |
| atob | Converts a byte to binary notation. |
| itob | Integer to binary notation. |
| btoa | Binary notation to its equivalent byte. |
| btoi | Binary notation to an integer. |
| xtob | Hex to binary notation. |
| btox | Binary to hex notation. |
| dump16 | Dumps 16 bytes in hex and ASCII. |

## rset

### ( width, destination, source )

*Description:*   By default, character data are always left-justified within a string. Sometimes, however, it's desirable to place the text at the right end of a field, as when aligning columns of figures on a report. rset performs this operation, taking the text from source and moving it to the right side of a field of the specified width in the destination array. It gets its name from the BASIC function that does the same thing.

*Parameters:*

> width is an integer specifying the number of characters in the receiving field. (This function uses one byte more than width for the null terminator.)
>
> destination is the name of a character array that will receive the right-justified results of rset. It must be at least one byte larger than width.
>
> source is the name of the character array containing the text that will be right-shifted.

*Type of Value Returned:*   None (results contained in destination).

*Other Functions Called:*   strlen.

*Remarks:*   It is permissible to name the same character array as both the source and the destination, in which case the data will be shifted within the same string. It is your responsibility to make sure that the receiving array is at least one byte larger than width to accommodate the null terminator, and that the text to be shifted will fit within width. The maximum number of bytes in any field processed by rset is 80, unless you change the array size for tmp in the function.

```
rset ( width, dest src )    /* right-justify string */
int     width;
char    dest [], src [];
{
    int     sp, dp;
    char    tmp [ 80 ];

        for ( dp = 0; dp < width; dp++ )
            tmp [ dp ] = ´ ´;                    /* fill with spaces */
        tmp [ width ] = ´0´;
        sp = strlen ( src );
        dp = width;
        while ( sp >= 0 )
            tmp [ dp-- ] = src [ sp-- ];    /* copy to temp string */
        dest [ width ] = ´ .´;
        strcpy ( dest, tmp );                   /* final copy */
```

## lset

### ( destination, source )

*Description:*   The lset function is the opposite of rset. It removes the leading white space (SPACE characters and TABs) from the source string and places the results—a string whose first visible character is in the 0th position—into the destination character array. In other words, it shifts the contents of source to the extreme left of destination, thus achieving left justification of the text. Note that left justification is the norm in text processing, so lset is seldom needed. Like rset, it takes its name from the BASIC function that does the same thing.

*Parameters:*

destination is a character array that will hold the left-shifted results when lset completes.
source is a character array containing the string to be left-shifted.

*Type of Value Returned:*   None (results in destination).

*Other Functions Called:*   None.

*Remarks:*   The function has no effect if the data are already left-justified in source, except that identical data will be in destination when it returns. Both source and destination can be the same array, in which case the data are merely "slid" to the left end of the array.

```
lset ( dest, src )          /* remove leading white */
char *dest, *src;           /* space from a string  */
{
    while ( isspace ( *src ))
        src++;
    while ( *dest++ = *src++ )
        ;
}
```

## stround

### ( places, destination, source )

*Description:*   This function reworks a character arrray of digits so that it will have a specified number of decimal places, rounded as appropriate. For example, if the numeric field in source is 3.1415927 and the places parameter is 4, stround returns 3.1416 in the destination array.

   Note that this function operates on character arrays containing digits, and not on numeric variables. Permissible characters are the digits, the " + " and "-" signs, and a decimal point. If the source string contains other alphanumerics, stround will usually return them as is in the destination string, but since this is obviously an error, the results of the function should be viewed with suspicion. stround does not report errors.

   The stround function always rounds upward in the direction of absolute value; -3.14159 rounds to -3.1416, not -3.1415. If the source string contains fewer than the specified number of decimal places, stround pads it with trailing zeros, so that 12.3 reformatted to three places is 12.300. In the case of very small values such as 0.00009 rounded to fewer decimal places—say, three—stround returns 0.000. When the first character of the string of digits is a decimal point, the function places a leading zero before it. A leading plus sign is ignored and not returned, but a leading minus sign is returned as such.

   stround is useful for creating reports that have columns of figures with the decimals aligned, and for other purposes requiring a fixed number of decimal places. You should note that the function returns string fields that are left-justified; use rset to right-shift the results, if appropriate.

*Parameters:*

   places is an integer specifying the number of decimal places the result should have.
   destination is the name of the character array in which stround returns the result.
   source is the name of the string containing the character-data value to be rounded.

*Type of Value Returned:*   None (results in destination).

*Other Functions Called:*   pos_of.

*Remarks:* The source string can contain up to 76 characters including a leading sign and a decimal point (see the second paragraph of Description for permissible characters). It's okay to name the same string as both the **source** and the **destination**, in which case the result replaces the original data in the array.

```
stround ( places, dest, src )     /* round numeric string */
int     places;
char    dest [], src [];
{
    char    work [ 80 ], sign;
    int     pivot, dp, i, length, n, np, carry, digit;

        for ( dp = 0; dp < 80; dp++ )
            work [ dp ] = '\0';
        carry = n = dp = 0;
        work [ dp++ ] = ' ';
        if (( sign = src [ n ] ) == '-' ) {    /* get sign if any */
            work [ dp++ ] = ' ';
            n++;
        }
        if ( src [ n ] == '.' )
            work [ dp++ ] = '0';
        if ( src [ n ] == '9' )
            work [ dp++ ] = ' ';
        while ( src [ n ] )                         /* copy to work */
            work [ dp++ ] = src [ n++ ];
        if ( places < 0 )                  /* if bad places parm */
            goto copy;
        length = strlen ( work );
        if (( n = pos_of ( '.', work )) == -1 ) {
            work [ length++ ] = '.';               /* if an integer */
            n = length;
        }
        if (( np = strlen ( &work [ n + 1 ] )) == places )
            goto copy;
        if ( np < places ) {                       /* pad with 0's */
            dp = length;
            for ( i = 0; i < ( places - np ); i++ )
                work [ dp++ ] = '0';
        } else {                                   /* round? */
            dp = n + places + 1;
            pivot = work [ dp ];
            work [ dp-- ] = '\0';                   /* truncate */
            if ( pivot < '5' )
                goto copy;                          /* that's all */
            carry = 1;
```

```
        do {
            if (( digit = work [ dp ] ) == '.' )
                digit = work [ --dp ];
            if ( ++digit >= '0' && digit <= '9' ) {
                work [ dp-- ] = digit;
                carry = 0;
            } else
                work [ dp-- ] = '0';
        } while ( carry == 1 && dp > 0 );
        dp++;
        if ( carry == 1 ) {                 /* final carry */
            if ( sign != '-' )
                work [ dp ] = '1';
            else {
                work [ dp++ ] = ' ';
                work [  dp  ] = '1';
            }
        }
    }
copy:   length = strlen ( work );
        for ( dp = 0; dp <= length + 1; dp++ )
            dest [ dp ] = '\0';
        dp = n = 0;
        if ( sign == '-' )                  /* insert sign */
            dest [ dp++ ] = sign;
        do {
            if (( digit = work [ n++ ] ) != ' ' )
                dest [ dp++ ] = digit;
        } while ( digit );
}
```

## dollars

### ( size, destination, source )

*Description:*   Business applications programs almost always require monetary output, yet about the only languages that make any provision for formatting dollars-and-cents amounts are COBOL and the better versions of BASIC. With this function, C joins them as a powerful business language, as well as being good for a lot of other things. The dollars function accepts any amount as character data, rounds it to the nearest penny, and returns the representation of that amount in customary monetary notation in the destination character array. It even inserts commas, carries a leading dollar sign, and right-justifies it within a field whose width is given by size. For example, 12345.668 is returned as $12,345.67, and -9841.5962 as $-9,841.60.

*Parameters:*

size is an integer specifying the width of the character field that will hold the result.

destination is the name of a character array that will receive the monetary-formatted result.

source is a character array containing the source data quantity as a string of ASCII digits.

*Type of Value Returned:*   None (results in destination).

*Other Functions Called:*   strlen, stround, rset.

*Remarks:*   The source field can contain up to 47 digits plus a decimal point and an optional sign. The destination field must be large enough to accommodate the result, which is 80 bytes for a 47-byte source field. In general, the same rules apply for this function as for stround, with one exception: regardless of the value of the size parameter, dollars always returns a field of the minimum width to hold the result. That is, if you pass a small value for size (say 2) and a large number, the result will be of exactly the width needed to hold it.

```
dollars ( size, dest, src )              /* monetary notation */
int     size;
char    dest [], src [];
{
    int     width, length, sp, dp, count;
    char    work [ 80 ], digit;

        stround ( 2, dest, src );
        length = strlen ( dest );
        width = (( length - 4 ) / 3 ) + length + 1;
        rset ( width, work, dest );
        for ( dp = 0; dp <= width; dp++ )
            dest [ dp ] = ' ';
        dest [ width + 1 ] = '\0';
        for ( count = 0, sp = dp = width;      /* move dec part */
                count < 3; count++ )
            dest [ dp-- ] = work [ sp-- ];
        count = -2;
        while (( digit = work [ sp-- ] ) != ' ' &&
                digit != '-' ) {
            if ( ++count == 3 ) {
                dest [ dp-- ] = ',';           /* insert commas */
                count = 0;
            }
            dest [ dp-- ] = digit;             /* copy digits */
        }
        if ( digit == '-' )
            dest [ dp-- ] = digit;
        dest [ dp ] = '$';                     /* dollar sign */
        if (( length = strlen ( work )) > size )
            size = length;
        rset ( size , dest, dest );
}
```

## ( destination, length, amount )

***Description:*** This is a truly nifty function which, though long, is an invaluable aid to those whose programs write monetary amounts on bank checks and other such documents. In brief, it works like this: you pass it the name of a character array, the array's length, and an amount such as 3025.79, and the function loads the destination character arrary with the text.

```
******* THREE THOUSAND TWENTY FIVE DOLLARS AND 79 CENTS
```

Thus, it translates a monetary amount into English words. Note that the left end of the field is padded with leading asterisks (*) to prevent tampering with the check, in accordance with standard practice. The text is always right-justified to the specified length, and the leading asterisks begin at the first (0th) position of the array and use up all free positions, leaving one space before the first text character.

ck__wtr is useful for any amount of money up to $99,999.99. If the amount exceeds that, it returns a 0 integer to indicate that it was unable to process the amount, and the destination string is empty (begins with a null terminator). For valid amounts, it returns an integer 1 to indicate successful completion, and that the text is in the destination array.

***Parameters:***

> destination is a character array where the function will write the amount in English words.
> length is an integer value specifying the length of the destination array.
> amount is a numeric double giving the amount to be translated into English words. The function will automatically round it to the nearest penny.

***Type of Value Returned:*** Integer (0 if not successful, 1 if it is).

***Other Functions Called:*** lset, rset (from this book), sprintf, strlen, strcpy (from the standard library).

***Remarks:*** The destination string must be long enough to hold any results that ck__wtr generates; an 80-byte array is sufficient for amounts up to $99,999.99. The function does not check to see whether it has exceeded the specified length, with the consequence that if the array is too short for the results, the function may clobber adjacent data areas and return garbage without a Ø indicator. Also, the function does not contemplate handling negative amounts (since checks are not written for such amounts) and will return unpredictable results if given an **amount** less than $0.00.

```
int ck_wtr ( dest, len, amt )     /* amount in English words */
char    dest [ ];                 /*     for check writing    */
int     len;
double amt;
{
    char    val [ 9 ], t, h, th, tth;
    int     vl, s, p = 0;

        dest [ 0 ] = '\0';              /* clear dest string */
        if ( amt > 99999.99 )
            return ( 0 );               /* amount too large */
        sprintf ( val, "%.2f", amt );
        if (( vl = strlen ( val )) == 3 || ( vl == 4 && val [ 0 ] == '0' )) {
            strcpy ( dest, "ZERO DOLLARS AND " );
            goto cents;
        }
        if ( vl == 4 && val [ 0 ] == '1' ) {
            strcpy ( dest, "ONE DOLLAR AND " );
            goto cents;
        }
        while (( vl = strlen ( val )) > 3 ) {          /* main loop */
            t = h = th = tth = 0;
            switch ( vl ) {                 /* set boolean for magnitude */
                case 5: t = 1;
                        break;
                case 6: h = 1;
                        break;
                case 7: th = 1;
                        break;
                case 8: tth = 1;
                        break;
            }
            if ( tth || t ) {                   /* ten thousands or tens */
                switch ( val [ 0 ] ) {
                    case '9':   strcpy ( &dest [ p ], "NINETY " );
                                break;
                    case '8':   strcpy ( &dest [ p ], "EIGHTY " );
                                break;
                    case '7':   strcpy ( &dest [ p ], "SEVENTY " );
                                break;
                    case '6':   strcpy ( &dest [ p ], "SIXTY " );
                                break;
                    case '5':   strcpy ( &dest [ p ], "FIFTY " );
                                break;
                    case '4':   strcpy ( &dest [ p ], "FORTY " );
                                break;
                    case '3':   strcpy ( &dest [ p ], "THIRTY " );
                                break;
                    case '2':   strcpy ( &dest [ p ], "TWENTY " );
                                break;
                    case '1':   val [ 0 ] = ' ';
                                lset ( val, val );
```

```
                                    switch ( val [ 0 ] ) {
                                        case '9': strcpy ( &dest [ p ], "NINETEEN " );
                                                break;
                                        case '8': strcpy ( &dest [ p ], "EIGHTEEN " );
                                                break;
                                        case '7': strcpy ( &dest [ p ], "SEVENTEEN " );
                                                break;
                                        case '6': strcpy ( &dest [ p ], "SIXTEEN " );
                                                break;
                                        case '5': strcpy ( &dest [ p ], "FIFTEEN " );
                                                break;
                                        case '4': strcpy ( &dest [ p ], "FOURTEEN " );
                                                break;
                                        case '3': strcpy ( &dest [ p ], "THIRTEEN " );
                                                break;
                                        case '2': strcpy ( &dest [ p ], "TWELVE " );
                                                break;
                                        case '1': strcpy ( &dest [ p ], "ELEVEN " );
                                                break;
                                        case '0': strcpy ( &dest [ p ], "TEN " );
                                                break;
                                    }
                                    goto cont;
                        }
                while ( dest [ p ] )
                        p++;
                val [ 0 ] = ' ';
                lset ( val, val );                    /* shift left 1 digit */
        }
        switch ( val [ 0 ] ) {                              /* units */
            case '9':    strcpy ( &dest [ p ], "NINE " );
                    break;
            case '8':    strcpy ( &dest [ p ], "EIGHT " );
                    break;
            case '7':    strcpy ( &dest [ p ], "SEVEN " );
                    break;
            case '6':    strcpy ( &dest [ p ], "SIX " );
                    break;
            case '5':    strcpy ( &dest [ p ], "FIVE " );
                    break;
            case '4':    strcpy ( &dest [ p ], "FOUR " );
                    break;
            case '3':    strcpy ( &dest [ p ], "THREE " );
                    break;
            case '2':    strcpy ( &dest [ p ], "TWO " );
                    break;
            case '1':    strcpy ( &dest [ p ], "ONE " );
                    break;
        }
cont:       while ( dest [ p ] )
                p++;
        if ( h && val [ 0 ] != '0' ) {
            strcpy ( &dest [ p ], "HUNDRED " );
            while ( dest [ p ] )
                p++;
        }
        if ( th || tth ) {
            strcpy ( &dest [ p ], "THOUSAND " );
            while ( dest [ p ] )
                p++;
        }
```

```
            val [ 0 ] = ( val [ 0 ] == '.' ) ? '.' : ' ';
            lset ( val, val );                    /* shift out left value */
        }                                         /*  end of while loop */
        strcpy ( &dest [ p ], "DOLLARS AND " );
cents:  while ( dest [ p ] )                              /* copy cents */
            p++;
        val [ 0 ] = ' ';
        if ( val [ 1 ] == '.' )
            val [ 1 ] = ' ';
        lset ( val, val );
        strcpy ( &dest [ p ], val );
        while ( dest [ p ] )
            p++;
        strcpy ( &dest [ p ], " CENTS\0" );
        rset ( len, dest, dest );
        p = 0;
        while ( dest [ p + 1 ] == ' ' )
            dest [ p++ ] = '*';                   /* fill with leading *'s */
        return ( 1 );
}
```

## atox

### ( result, byte )

*Description:*   This function and all those that follow in this chapter are useful chiefly in writing system utilities that inspect the contents of memory or disks and for disassemblers, debuggers, and other programs that reveal otherwise nonprintable data. atox takes any 8-bit byte and converts it to two ASCII characters representing the byte's bit pattern in hexadecimal notation, placing the result in a 3-byte null-terminated string. The byte can be an ASCII character, a control byte, machine language, or any other 8-bit configuration.

*Parameters:*

result is the name of a character array at least three bytes in length that will receive the ASCII-formatted hexadecimal result.
byte is the single byte to be converted to hex notation.

*Type of Value Returned:*   None (modifies result).

*Other Functions Called:*   None.

```
atox ( result, byte )    /* char to hex notation */
char    result [], byte;
{
    char    work [ 2 ];
    int     i, val;

        result [ 2 ] = ´ .´;
        for ( i = 0; i < 2; i++ )
            work [ i ] = byte;
        work [ 0 ] >>= 4;                    /* high-order nibble */
        for ( i = 0; i < 2; i++ ) {
            work [ i ] &= 0x0f;
            if (( val = work [ i ] < 10 )
                result [ i ] = val + ´0´;      /* convert */
            else                               /*    to    */
                result [ i ] = val + ´A´ - 10; /*   hex    */
        }
}
```

## itox

## ( destination, value )

*Description:* This function, useful mainly in systems programming applications, accepts a signed integer value and returns its equivalent hexadecimal notation as ASCII characters in the destination array. itox is specifically intended for microcomputers, in which integers are universally 16-bit (2-byte) values with the components in reverse order; that is, low-order byte first, followed by the high-order byte on the right. Such integers have a range of $-32768$ to $+32767$, with the minus sign denoted by the highest order bit being set to 1. Thus, a negative integer always has a first hex digit of 8 or greater, and positive numbers have a first hex digit of 7 or less. The bit pattern "wraps" at the highest integer value, so that $+32767$ is hex 7FFF, while $-32768$ is represented by hex 8000 and $-1$ is hex FFFF. Note that although integers are internally represented in low-byte/high-byte order, their hex equivalents are customarily written in standard high-byte/low-byte order, and the results of itox follow this convention.

*Parameters:*

> destination is the name of an array that will receive the hex representation as ASCII characters.
> value is the signed integer numeric variable to be converted to hex.

*Type of Value Returned:* None (results in destination).

*Other Functions Called:* atox.

*Remarks:* For unsigned integers such as addresses, use utox presented in the following section.

```
itox ( dest, value )              /* signed integer to hex */
char    dest [];
int     value;
{
    union {
        int     nbr;
        char    str [ 2 ];
    } parm;

        parm.nbr = value;
        atox ( &dest [ 0 ], parm.str [ 1 ] );
        atox ( &dest [ 2 ], parm.str [ 0 ] );
}
```

**utox**

## ( destination, value )

*Description:*   This function is similar to itox, except that it converts an *un*signed 16-bit integer variable into a string containing the equivalent hex notation as ASCII characters. Like itox, it applies to microcomputers, in which the range of unsigned integers is Ø through 65535. These values are used most often for counters and memory addresses.

*Parameters:*

destination is the name of a character array that will receive the hex notation as ASCII characters.

value is an unsigned integer numeric variable to be converted to hex.

*Type of Value Returned:*   None (results returned in destination).

*Other Functions Called:*   atox.

*Remarks:*   For signed integers, use itox.

```
utox ( dest, value )          /* unsigned integer to hex */
char          dest [];
unsigned int    value;
{
    union {
        unsigned int      nbr;
        char              str [ 2 ];
    } parm;

        parm.nbr = value;
        atox ( &dest [ 0 ], parm.str [ 1 ] );
        atox ( &dest [ 2 ], parm.str [ 0 ] );
}
```

## ( hex )

*Description:*   This function is the opposite of atox in that it returns the 8-bit byte represented by a two-digit hexadecimal string. All 8-bit patterns are given by the hex digits Ø–9 and A–F, which must be ASCII characters within the parameter string hex. If xtoa detects any other characters within the string, it returns a byte value of 255 to indicate an error. (*Note:* This error code is potentially confusing, since the function also returns an entirely valid code 255 when the hex parameter string contains the hex value FF.)

*Parameters:*   hex is a 2-byte string containing the hexadecimal notation (as ASCII characters) that is to be converted to a byte.

*Type of Value Returned:*   Character.

*Other Functions Called:*   upshift.

*Remarks:*   The lowercase hex digits (a–f) can be used instead of their uppercase counterparts. The hex string must *always* contain two hex digits; a leading zero must be explicitly included (i.e., for hex value 5, pass Ø5 and not simply 5).

```c
char xtoa ( hex )                /* hex notation to byte */
char    hex [];
{
    char    result, work;
    int     p;

        upshift ( hex );
        for ( p = 0; p < 2; p++ ) {
            work = hex [ p ];
            if ( work >= ´0´ && work <= ´9´ )
                work -= ´0´;
            else {
                if ( work >= ´A´ && work <= ´F´ )
                    work -= ´A´ - 10;
                else
                    return ( 255 );      /* error */
            }
            if ( p == 0 )
                result = ( work <<= 4 );
            else
                result |= work;
        }
        return ( result );
}
```

## xtoi

### ( hex )

*Description:*   This function is similar to **xtoa**, except that it converts a string of four hex digits (0−9 and A−F) into a 16-bit integer variable. The hex digits must be ASCII characters in high-to-low order within a character array. The return value is in the customary low-to-high format of microcomputer-based integers (see the relevant discussion under **itox** above).

*Parameters:*   **hex** is the name of a character array containing ASCII hexadecimal digits to be converted to an integer.

*Type of Value Returned:*   Integer (signed or unsigned: see Remarks below).

*Other Functions Called:*   **xtoa**.

*Remarks:*   You can use **xtoi** for both signed and unsigned integers, since the declared type of the receiving variable determines how the program interprets its value. Unlike **xtoa**, this function does not return an error indicator for invalid hex digits in the source string. Therefore, it is your responsibility to ensure that the hex values passed to it are legitimate, lest **xtoi** return dubious results. Also, you must explicitly pass leading zeros in the hex source string in order to comply with the mandatory four-digit rule; for example, pass Ø12F and not 12F, since the latter will return an erroneous result.

```
int xtoi ( hex )          /* hex to integer */
char    hex [];
{
    union {
         int    nbr;
         char   str [ 2 ];
    } result;
    int        p;
    char       temp [ 2 ];

        for ( p = 2; p < 4; p++ )
            temp [ p - 2 ] = hex [ p ];
        result.str [ 0 ] = xtoa ( temp );
        for ( p = 0; p < 2; p++ )
            temp [ p ] = hex [ p ];
        result.str [ 1 ] = xtoa ( temp );
        return ( result.nbr );
}
```

**atob**

## ( binary, byte )

*Description:* atob accepts an ASCII (or other 8-bit) byte and returns its equivalent binary representation as a string. This string consists of a combination of eight Øs and 1s in high-to-low (left-to-right) order, followed by a null terminator, for a total of nine characters. It is useful in systems programming applications that entail viewing bit patterns.

*Parameters:*

> binary is the name of a string that will receive the results. It must have at least nine elements.
> byte is the 8-bit byte (usually type char) that is to be converted to binary.

*Type of Value Returned:* None (results in binary array).

*Other Functions Called:* None.

```
atob ( binary, byte )            /* byte to binary notation */
char    binary [], byte;
{
    int     p, mask;

        binary [ 8 ] = '\0';
        for ( p = 7, mask = 1; p >= 0; p-- ) {
            binary [ p ] = (( byte & mask ) >= 1 ) ? '1' : '0';
            mask *= 2;
        }
}
```

## ( binary, value )

*Description:*  itob resembles itox, except that it returns an 18-byte string showing the binary format of the integer passed in the value parameter. The integer may be signed or unsigned.

*Parameters:*

> binary is the name of a character array that will receive the binary notation as ASCII characters. It must have at least 18 elements to accommodate the result.
> value is a signed or unsigned integer to be converted into its equivalent binary notation.

*Type of Value Returned:*  None (results in binary).

*Other Functions Called:*  atob.

*Remarks:*  The result of itob is two 8-byte character fields separated by a space and terminated by a null. The leftmost bit of the binary result is the most significant, following standard notation conventions.

```
itob ( binary, value )              /* integer to binary */
char    binary [];
int     value;
{
    union {
        int     nbr;
        char    str [ 2 ];
    } parm;

        parm.nbr = value;
        atob ( &binary [ 0 ], parm.str [ 1 ] );
        atob ( &binary [ 9 ], parm.str [ 0 ] );
        binary [ 8 ] = ' ';
}
```

## btoa

## ( binary )

*Description:* btoa is similar to xtoa except that it converts an 8-digit string of binary digits (1s and Øs) into an 8-bit byte, which it returns as the result.

*Parameters:* binary is the name of the string containing the binary notation as ASCII digits 1 and Ø.

*Type of Value Returned:* An 8-bit byte, nominally of the standard char type in C.

*Other Functions Called:* None.

*Remarks:* Any character in the binary string that is not a 1 is interpreted as a Ø.

```
char btoa ( binary )                    /* binary to byte */
char    binary [];
{
    int      p;
    char     byte;

        byte = 0;
        for ( p = 0; p < 8; p++ ) {
            byte <<= 1;
            if ( binary [ p ] == '1' )
                byte |= 1;
        }
        return ( byte );
}
```

## ( binary )

***Description:*** btoi is similar to xtoi, except that it develops an integer variable based upon the contents of a string containing sixteen binary digits in ASCII. This binary string must consist of two fields, each of eight ASCII digits 1 or Ø, with a space (or other cosmetic character) separating the fields; for example, the binary string "ØØØØ1111  1111ØØØ1" returns the integer 4Ø81.

***Parameters:*** binary is a string literal or the name of a character array containing the binary value as ASCII digits 1 and Ø.

***Type of Value Returned:*** Integer (may be signed or unsigned, as the receiving variable determines how the program interprets it).

***Other Functions Called:*** btoa.

***Remarks:*** Any binary digit that is not a 1 is interpreted as a Ø.

```
int btoi ( binary )          /* binary to integer */
char    binary [];
{
    union {
        int     nbr;
        char    str [ 2 ];
    } parm;

        parm.str [ 1 ] = btoa ( &binary [ 0 ] );
        parm.str [ 0 ] = btoa ( &binary [ 9 ] );
        return ( parm.nbr );
}
```

## xtob

## ( destination, source )

**Description:**  Hexadecimal is a shorthand form of binary in which there is a direct correlation between each 4-bit binary pattern and a corresponding "hex" digit: binary 0001 is hex 1, 1001 is 9, 1010 is A, etc. The purpose of the xtob function is to expand a pair of hex digits in the source string into its equivalent 8-bit binary pattern and return the result in destination.

**Parameters:**

> destination is the name of a character array (with a minimum length of nine elements) that will receive the binary result.
> source is a string containing the two hex digits to be converted to binary.

**Type of Value Returned:**  None (result is in destination).

**Other Functions Called:**  xtoa, atob.

**Remarks:**  Both parameters may be the same array, in which case the binary result replaces the hex source data.

---

```
xtob ( dest, src )        /* hex to binary */
char    dest [], src [];
{
        atob ( dest, xtoa ( src ) );
}
```

---

**btox**

# ( destination, source )

*Description:*   This function has an effect that is the exact opposite of xtob in the last section; it converts an 8-bit ASCII pattern of binary digits into the equivalent pair of hex digits.

*Parameters:*

   destination is the name of a character array with a minimum length of 3 bytes that will receive the hex result.

   source is the string containing the eight ASCII binary digits to be converted to hex.

*Type of Value Returned:*   None (results returned in destination).

*Other Functions Called:*   btoa, atox.

*Remarks:*   Both parameters can be the same character array, in which case the hex result replaces the binary source data.

---

```
btox ( dest, src )          /* binary to hex */
char    dest [], src [];
{
        atox ( dest, btoa ( src ) );
}
```

---

## dump16

( block )

*Description:* This function displays a standard dump format for 16 bytes of data contained in block, which can be either a character array or a pointer to memory. Standard dump format creates two regions on each line. The first region is 48 bytes in length and consists of the hex digits for each of the 16 bytes. There is a space character preceding each pair of hex digits. Following the sixteenth hex pair are four spaces, then the ASCII representations of the 16 bytes. When a byte value is outside the normal range of ASCII printable characters (i.e., less than 32 or greater than 126), a period is substituted in the character region to prevent the screen from doing bizarre things.

This function is useful in systems programming for examining chunks of memory and disk sectors, and for peeking into other dark corners of the computer.

*Parameters:* block is a character array containing the 16 bytes to be dumped, or a pointer to the 16-byte block of memory you want to examine.

*Type of Value Returned:* Nonc.

*Other Functions Called:* atox.

```
dump16 ( block )              /* formatted 16 byte dump line */
char    block [];
{
    char    hex [ 3 ], text [ 17 ], byte;
    int     p;

    for ( p = 0; p < 16; p++ ) {
        byte = block [ p ];
        atox ( hex, byte );
        printf ( " %s", hex;
        if ( byte > 31 && byte < 127 )
            text [ p ] = byte;
        else
            text [ p ] = ;.;;
    }
    text [ 16 ] = ´ .´;
    printf ( "    %s\n", text );
}
```

# CHAPTER **3**

# USING ANSI.SYS ON THE IBM PC AND COMPATIBLE MACHINES

*T*he functions in this chapter exploit the ANSI.SYS device driver that comes with PC-DOS/MS-DOS to furnish a library of screen and keyboard control functions for the IBM PC and its "clones" (Compaq, Columbia, Tandy, and so forth). In order to utilize them, it's necessary to boot the machine with a CONFIG.SYS file containing the statement

DEVICE = ANSI.SYS

which automatically loads the device driver. Obviously, the ANSI.SYS file must be present on the boot diskette. If you are writing software for sale, it will be necessary for your package to load this device driver in your customers' systems in order for your software to utilize the screen functions.

The basic functions correspond with the facilities available through ANSI.SYS, and merely invoke them in C. Having done that, we then embark on a series of enhanced functions: for example, drawing stylized rectangles useful in windowing or as menu boundaries, placing the cursor at a specified point and writing text, etc., all of which contribute to the creation of friendly (or at least attractive) user interfaces.

Note that Chapter 4 presents a number of functions that are similar to those given here, but do not require ANSI.SYS. The advantage in using ANSI.SYS is that it's quite simple to do sophisticated things with the machine. The advantages of the functions in Chapter 4 are that you don't have to deal with this external device driver, and they are faster.

The following lists the functions in this chapter by name and gives a brief synopsis of what each one does.

### Basic group

| | |
|---|---|
| cls | Clear screen, home cursor. |
| ceol | Clear to end of line. |
| locate | Place cursor at specified row/column. |
| scp | Store cursor's current position. |
| rcp | Restore cursor to previous position. |
| curpos | Report the cursor's present position. |
| scrnmode | Set the screen mode. |
| sgr | Set the graphics rendition (reverse video, foreground/ background, etc.) |
| fkey | Assigns a command to a function key. |
| comkey | Assigns a command to a text key. |
| chkey | Changes character generated by a key. |

### Enhanced group

| | |
|---|---|
| ctr40 | Center text on 40-column screen. |
| ctr80 | Center text on 80-column screen. |
| place | Place cursor at row/column, write text. |
| box | Draw a rectangle on the text screen. |

# Basic group

## cls ()

*Description:*   Clears the screen of all contents and homes the cursor in the upper left corner.

*Parameters:*   None.

*Type of Value Returned:*   None.

*Other Functions Called:*   None.

*Remarks:*   Corresponds to ED in ANSI.SYS.

```
cls ()      /* clear screen */
{
    printf ( "%c[2J", 27 );
}
```

## ceol ()

*Description:*   Clears the line from the current cursor position to the right edge of the screen, inclusive. ceol stands for "clear to end of line."

*Parameters:*   None.

*Type of Value Returned:*   None.

*Other Functions Called:*   None.

*Remarks:*   Corresponds to EL in ANSI.SYS. (*Note:* Both the IBM and Compaq DOS manuals contain a typo in specifying this ANSI.SYS command: should be uppercase "K").

```
ceol ()                          /* clear to end of line */
{
    printf ( "%c[K", 27 );
}
```

## locate

**( row, column )**

*Description:*   Places the cursor at the specified row and column on the display screen.

*Parameters:*

   row is the row number (1−25).
   column is the column number (1−40 or 1−80).

*Type of Value Returned:*   None.

*Other Functions Called:*   None.

*Remarks:*   Corresponds to CUP in ANSI.SYS. locate does not verify that the row and column numbers are within valid ranges. This is your responsibility. Out-of-range values may crash the program or cause other problems.

```
locate ( row, col )          /*  position cursor at row, col  */
int       row, col;
{
    printf ( "%c[%d;%dH", 27, row, col );
}
```

## scp ()

*Description:* Stores the current location of the cursor so that it can later be restored to that position (by rcp). scp and rcp are paired functions. An example of their use is a situation in which you need to move the cursor to a status line to display an error message, then put the cursor back where it was. Call scp to save the current location, display the message, and then call rcp to restore the cursor to its original position.

*Parameters:* None.

*Type of Value Returned:* None.

*Other Functions Called:* None.

*Remarks:* Corresponds to SCP in ANSI.SYS. This function does not report the row/column cursor address back to the calling program; for that, see curpos.

```
scp ()           /* save current position of cursor  */
{
    printf ( "%c[s", 27 );
}
```

## rcp ()

*Description:* Restores the cursor to the position saved by a previous call to scp. See scp for a discussion of these paired functions.

*Parameters:* None.

*Type of Value Returned:* None.

*Other Functions Called:* None.

*Remarks:* Corresponds to RCP in ANSI.SYS.

---

```
rcp ()          /* restore cursor to position
                    saved by 'scp' function          */
{
    printf ( "%c[u", 27 );
}
```

---

## curpos

## ( row, col )

***Description:*** Reports the cursor's present row/column location to the calling program. This function is similar to scp, except that it returns the cursor coordinates instead of saving them at the system level (thus, rcp does not accurately restore the cursor after a call to curpos). The purpose of curpos is to enable the program to determine the cursor location, presumably to take some action based on where it is. As an example, if the cursor is in row 25, you might want to do something special to prevent the screen from scrolling the next time the user presses the ENTER key.

***Parameters:*** Addresses of two integer variables representing the row and column. Use the address operator ("&") in the function call, as in

```
curpos ( &row, &col );
```

***Type of Value Returned:*** Alters the values of the parameters whose addresses are passed. Thus, curpos indirectly returns its results.

***Other Functions Called:*** None from this book.

***Remarks:*** Corresponds to DSR in ANSI.SYS. The line bearing the remark "/* direct console input */" contains a function ci () which is used in DeSmet C. Other C compilers might use a different name for the function that furnishes direct input (not echoed to the display). Check your compiler's documentation.

```
curpos ( row, col )          /* report current cursor position */
int     *row, *col;
{
    char    reply [ 8 ], coord [ 3 ];
    int     s, d;

        printf ( "%c[6n", 27 );
        for ( s = 0; s < 8; s++ )
            reply [ s ] = ci ();      /* direct console input */
        coord [ 2 ] = '\0';
        for ( s = 2, d = 0; d < 2; s++, d++ )
            coord [ d ] = reply [ s ];
        *row = atoi ( coord );
        for ( s = 5, d = 0; d < 2; s++, d++ )
            coord [ d ] = reply [ s ];
        *col = atoi ( coord );
}
```

# scrnmode

## ( parm )

*Description:*   Use this function to establish the basic operating characteristics of the display screen. The options are listed below.

*Parameters:*   An integer indicating one of the following modes:

Ø. 40 × 25 monochrome
1. 40 × 25 color text
2. 80 × 25 monochrome
3. 80 × 25 color text
4. 320 × 200 color graphics

5. 320 × 200 monographics
6. 640 × 200 monographics
7. Disable wrap at end of line
8. Enable wrap at end of line

*Type of Value Returned:*   None.

*Other Functions Called:*   None.

*Remarks:*   Combines the SM and RM commands under ANSI.SYS. The "wrap" in options 7 and 8 above refers to the fate of characters typed at the right edge of the screen. When wrap is enabled, the line continues at the left end of the next row; when disabled, characters typed off the edge of the screen are lost.

You might wish to avoid "magic numbers" by using #define statements to assign meaningful labels to the modes. Example:

```
#define C8Ø×25    3
scrnmode (C8Ø×25);
```

```
scrnmode ( parm )          /* set screen mode */
int         parm;
{
    switch ( parm ) {
        case 8:     printf ( "%c[=7h", 27 );
                    break;
        default:    printf ( "%c[=%dl", 27, parm );
                    break;
    }
}
```

# sgr

## ( attribute, foreground, background )

*Description:* The name of this function is an abbreviation of "Set Graphics Rendition," a somewhat obscure term borrowed directly from Microsoft, the makers of PC-DOS and MS-DOS. What this function does is to give you control over the attributes (appearance characteristics) and the foreground and background colors of text appearing on the screen. Because I have taken a few liberties with the parameters, it's best not to rely on your DOS manual (which isn't very helpful in this case anyway) for an explanation of what the function does, but instead to get your information about setting the "graphics rendition" here. This is quite a complex function and the explanation is, accordingly, long-winded; but it's not difficult to use and it's well worth learning for anyone who wants to create attractive displays.

sgr always expects three parameters, which we'll call attribute, foreground, and background, those being somewhat self-explanatory names. The establishment of an attribute or color via this function takes effect immediately and remains in effect until the next call. Each parameter has a "no-change" value (Ø) that tells sgr to leave its particular setting as is. For example, if the foreground color is red and you pass a set of parameters, the second of which (foreground) is Ø, the function will leave the foreground color as red.

Attributes refer to the appearance of the text on the screen, except for color. There are seven attribute parameters you can pass, the values and meanings of which are as follows:

Ø    No change to existing attributes
1    Restore normal video (white on black, or the usual monochrome video)
2    Highlight (high-intensity)
3    Underscore (applies to IBM monochrome display *only*)
4    Blinking text
5    Reverse video (foreground and background colors are reversed
6    Invisible (foreground is the same color as background)

You can only pass one attribute value per call to sgr, and the effect of successive calls is cumulative. For example, if you turn on blinking text with attribute value 4, all subsequent output to the screen will blink. If you later call sgr with attribute 5, blinking text still remains in effect, but it will also be in reverse video. The only way to cancel previous attributes is to pass a value of 1 (normal video). This not only turns off the former attributes, but also restores color to the normal light-on-black mode.

The `foreground` and `background` parameters control the colors of text subsequently appearing on the screen. There are nine color codes you can pass, and the same codes apply to both of the parameters. (*Note:* See the remarks for `scrnmode` concerning use of macros to avoid "magic numbers.") The codes are:

| | | |
|---|---|---|
| Ø No change | 3 Green | 6 Magenta |
| 1 Black | 4 Yellow | 7 Cyan |
| 2 Red | 5 Blue | 8 White |

For an example of using these parameters, suppose you want to set up a blinking field on the screen that has red letters on a white background. The call to accomplish this is

```
sgr ( 4, 2, 8 );
```

Now suppose that blinking red-on-white is still in effect and that you want subsequent output not to blink but still be red on white. For that you need to reestablish normal video with attribute 1 and then turn the color scheme back on. The call is

```
scr ( 1, 2, 8 );
```

This call turns off the blinking for subsequent output (although the text already blinking on the screen continues to do so), and it sets the colors back to red-on-white.

After some output in this color scheme, let's say you want to leave the letters red but change their background to black. This you can do with

```
scr (Ø, Ø, 1 );
```

which means "leave the attributes the same and don't change the foreground color, but make the background black."

As a matter of programming practice, one of the last official acts of a program that uses this function should be the call

```
sgr ( 1, Ø, Ø );
```

which restores the screen to its normal attributes and colors.

Even if you are using a monochrome monitor, you can achieve differing intensities of text by changing "colors," and thereby do shadow printing and create other effects on the display.

*Parameters:*  Three integer variables or literal numbers corresponding to attribute, foreground, and background discussed above.

***Type of Value Returned:***  None.

***Other Functions Called:***  None.

***Remarks:***  Invalid (out-of-range) parameters are ignored by sgr.

```c
sgr ( attrib, fg, bg )                /* set graphics rendition */
int    attrib, fg, bg;
{
        if ( attrib > 0 && attrib < 7 ) {
                printf ( "%c[", 27 );              /* control lead */
                switch ( attrib ) {
                        case 1: puts ( "0m" );     /* restore normal */
                                break;
                        case 2: puts ( "1m" );          /* highlight */
                                break;
                        case 3: puts ( "4m" );          /* underscore */
                                break;
                        case 4: puts ( "5m" );              /* blink */
                                break;
                        case 5: puts ( "7m" );      /* reverse video */
                                break;
                        case 6: puts ( "8m" );          /* invisible */
                                break;
                }
        }
        if ( fg > 0 && fg < 9 )      /* set foreground color */
                printf ( "%c[%dm", 27, fg + 29 );

        if ( bg > 0 && bg < 9 )      /* set background color */
                printf ( "%c[%dm", 27, bg + 39 );
}
```

## fkey

### ( key, command )

*Description:*   This routine furnishes a means for assigning a command line to any of the function keys F1–F10. As soon as **fkey** has executed, operation of the function key has the same effect as if the named command were typed at the keyboard. As an example, you might assign the DOS command

    dir b:/w

to key F10. Thereafter, any time you press F10, it's the same as typing the command. The function call to accomplish this is

    fkey ( 10, "dir b:/w" );

Command lines associated with the function keys can be anything: DOS commands, names of programs, BAT files, or whatever. There is, however, no provision for "plugging in" variables; the command line you assign to the function key will be executed exactly as is. Assignments made via this function remain in effect until:

1. The system is rebooted, or;
2. Another program runs that utilizes the function keys for its own purposes, such as Framework or Lotus 1-2-3, or;
3. You exercise **fkey** to give the same key a different meaning.

You can "undo" a function key assignment by passing a null string as the new command line in a call to **fkey**. To make the F10 key have *no* meaning, call the function with

    fkey ( 10, "" );

*Parameters:*

   **key** is an integer between 1 and 10 corresponding to the function key you want to make an assignment to.
   **command** is the text of the command line that will be executed when the function key is pressed.

*Type of Value Returned:*   None.

*Other Functions Called:*   None.

**Remarks:** If an invalid function key number is passed (outside the range of 1–10), **fkey** returns with no effect.

```
fkey ( key, cmd )       /* assign command to function key */
int     key;
char    cmd [ ];
{
        if ( key < 1 || key > 10 )
             return;                            /* invalid key    */
        printf ( "%c[0;", 27 );                 /* control lead   */
        printf ( "%d;", key + 58 );             /* fcn key value  */
        printf ( "%c%s%c", 34, cmd, 34 );          /* command     */
        puts ( ";13p" );                        /* end sentinel   */
}
```

## comkey

### ( key, command )

*Description:* comkey is similar to fkey (presented above), except that it assigns a command to a normally text-producing key. For example, I don't know about you, but I haven't much use for the tilde (˜) character, which is the value normally obtained by shifting the key between the quotes and ENTER on the IBM PC (note: This character is a unary operator in C). Supposing that our neglect of this character is mutual, we can assign it to assume a command function with comkey; let's say that when you press it, you want to see a wide directory listing from the A: drive, the same as typing the command.

    dir a:/w

The function call to accomplish this is

    comkey ('˜', "dir a:/w" );

An alternative that does the same thing is

    comkey ( 126, "dir a:/w" );

since the tilde character has the ASCII value 126. In other words, you can pass either the ASCII integer value of the character, or the character itself in single quotes. Having made the assignment via comkey, any time you press SHIFT and the tilde character, you'll get a directory listing of drive A:.

You can "undo" a command assignment by calling comkey and passing a null string, as in

    comkey ( 126, "" );

but there is an undesirable result; afterward, the affected key will have *no* value whatsoever. The better way to dismantle a command assignment and put the key back to its normal state is to use the chkey function discussed below.

*Parameters:*

key is an integer (variable or literal) expressing the ASCII code of the affected key, *or* the character itself in single quotes.

command is the text of the command line that will be executed when the assigned key is pressed.

***Type of Value Returned:*** None.

***Other Functions Called:*** None.

```
comkey ( key, cmd )              /* assign a command to a key */
int    key;
char   cmd [];
{
       printf ( "%c[", 27 );                /* control lead  */
       printf ( "%d;", key );               /* ascii value   */
       printf ( "%c%s%c", 34, cmd, 34 );    /* command       */
       puts ( ";13p" );                     /* end sentinel  */
}
```

## chkey

**( key, new )**

*Description:*   The `chkey` function changes the ASCII value of a key to something else, thereby changing the character the key generates. For an example, I'll pick once again on the tilde (˜) key, which was also the victim in the discussion of `comkey` above. Suppose you're writing some text in Spanish, which has the "enye" character (an "n" with a tilde above it). This character is not normally available from the keyboard, although it is within the character set of the IBM PC and presumably all clones as ASCII value 164. To reassign the tilde character to generate an "enye," issue the function call

        chkey ( 126, 164 );

or, in an equivalent form,

        chkey ( '˜', 164);

and thereafter (until the system is rebooted), pressing down SHIFT and typing the tilde will produce an "enye."

   Later, if you want to restore the key so that it produces a tilde again, you can call the function with

        chkey ( 164, 126 );

or

        chkey ( 164, '˜' );

   In the discussion of `comkey`, I mentioned that the best way to undo a command assignment is with `chkey`. If you have assigned a command to the tilde key, you can make the tilde itself again with the function call

        chkey ( 126, 126 );

which removes the command assignment from that ASCII code.

*Parameters:*

   `key` is the ASCII integer code or the character itself in single quotes that will be changed.
   `new` is the ASCII integer value of the new assignment to `key`.

*Type of Value Returned:*   None.

***Other Functions Called:*** None.

```
chkey ( key, new )       /* reassign value for a key */
int     key, new;
{
    printf ( "%c[", 27 );             /* control lead */
    printf ( "%d;%dp", key, new ); /* ascii value */
```

# Enhanced group

## ( row, text )

*Description:*   This is an enhanced screen-formatting function that centers a text item horizontally within the given row of a 40-column screen. It's handy for centering screen headings and that sort of thing because it saves you the trouble of figuring out how many characters the text unit has and then calculating where it belongs within the horizontal domain of the row.

*Parameters:*

row is an integer in the range 1–25 that gives the screen row where the text is to appear.
text is a string literal or the name of a character array containing the text to be centered.

*Type of Value Returned:*   None.

*Other Functions Called:*   strlen, locate.

*Remarks:*   ctr40 does not verify that the row number is within the valid range for the screen, nor that the text will fit within the 40 columns of the screen.

```
ctr40 ( row, text )          /*  center text in given row
                                 of 40-column screen       */
int     row;
char    text [];
{
    int    length, col;

        length = strlen ( text );
        col    = ( 40 - length ) / 2;
        locate ( row, col );
        puts ( text );
}
```

## ctr80

### ( row, text )

*Description:*   This function is identical to **ctr40**, except that it centers text on the given row of an 80-column display screen.

*Parameters:*

> **row** is an integer in the range 1–25 that gives the screen row where the text is to appear.
>
> **text** is a string literal or the name of a character array containing the text to be centered.

*Type of Value Returned:*   None.

*Other Functions Called:*   strlen, locate.

*Remarks:*   ctr80 does not verify that the row number is within the valid range for the screen, nor that the text will fit within the 80 columns of the screen.

```
ctr80 ( row, text )            /*  center text in given row
                                   of 80-column screen       */
int     row;
char    text [];
{
    int     length, col;

        length = strlen ( text );
        col    = ( 80 - length ) / 2;
        locate ( row, col );
        puts ( text );
}
```

## place

**( row, col, text )**

*Description:*  This function lets you place text anywhere on the screen by specifying the row and column position where it is to begin and the text that is to appear there. It is simply a combination of locate and puts, the purpose of which is to keep source programs more concise and readable when creating formatted screen displays.

*Parameters:*

row is the integer row number (1–25 ) where the text will begin.
col is the integer column number (1–40 or 1–80, depending on the screen mode) where the first letter of the text will appear.
text is a string literal or the name of a character array whose contents are to be displayed.

*Type of Value Returned:*  None.

*Other Functions Called:*  locate.

*Remarks:*  Does not verify that the screen address is within boundaries or that the text will fit on the display.

---

```
place ( row, col, text )     /* place text at row, col  */
int     row, col;
char    text [];
{
    locate ( row, col );
    puts ( text );
}
```

---

**box**

## ( style, ulr, ulc, lrr, lrc )

***Description:***   For software developers as well as those with a passion for neat, well-designed screen formats, this function is a godsend. It draws rectangular boxes in text mode and gives you six different styles to choose from. You can use it to outline menus, to fence functional areas within a display, to highlight sections of reports, and for all sorts of other things leading to highly professional layouts. All it takes is one line of code to create a box anywhere you need one.

A "box" is defined by its upper left and lower right corners in the context of this function, the corners occurring in row and column positions on the screen. For example, suppose you specify a box with its upper left corner (parameters ulr and ulc) at row 4, column 6, and its lower right corner (lrr and lrc) at row 8, column 15. The box will then appear something like this diagram:

The chief difference between the diagram and the actual box has to do with the matter of style. The style parameter determines the character set used to build the box image. If you look in the appendices of the BASIC manual that came with your computer, you will find the box-making characters. The following style table gives the decimal value (so that you can look it up) of the upper right corner's character.

| Style | ASCII | Description |
|-------|-------|-------------|
| 1 | 218 | Single line |
| 2 | 201 | Double line |
| 3 | 176 | Light shadow |
| 4 | 177 | Medium shadow |
| 5 | 178 | Dark shadow |
| 6 | 219 | Solid line |

*Parameters:*

> style is an integer variable or literal in the range 1–6 that selects
> the character set used to draw the box.
> ulr and ulc are the upper left row and column numbers of the box
> outline.
> lrr and lrc are the lower right row and column numbers of the box.

*Type of Value Returned:*  None.

*Other Functions Called:*  locate.

*Remarks:*  If the style parameter is invalid, the function defaults to
style 1 (single line). box does not verify that the specified dimensions
are within the screen boundaries.

```
box ( style, ulr, ulc, lrr, lrc )   /* draws a box in specified style */
int    style, ulr, ulc, lrr, lrc;   /* from upper left to lower right */
{
    register int    r, c;
    char            horiz, vert, tl, tr, br, bl;

        scp ();                      /* save cursor position */
        if ( style < 1 || style > 6 )
            style = 1;
        switch ( style ) {
            case 1: horiz = 196;     /* single-score box */
                    vert  = 179;
                    tl    = 218;     tr = 191;
                    br    = 217;     bl = 192;
                    break;
            case 2: horiz = 205;     /* double-score box */
                    vert  = 186;
                    tl    = 201;     tr = 187;
                    br    = 188;     bl  = 200;
                    break;
            case 3:                          /* light shadow box */
                    horiz = vert = tl = tr = br = bl = 176;
                    break;
            case 4:                          /* medium shadow box */
                    horiz = vert = tl = tr = br = bl = 177;
                    break;
            case 5:                          /* heavy shadow box */
                    horiz = vert = tl = tr = br = bl = 178;
                    break;
            case 6:                          /* solid box */
                    horiz = vert = tl = tr = br = bl = 219;
                    break;
        }  /* end of switch */
        locate ( ulr, ulc );
        putchar ( tl );
```

```c
for ( c = 1; c < ( lrc - ulc ); c++ )      /* top */
    putchar ( horiz );
putchar ( tr );

locate ( lrr, ulc );
putchar ( bl );
for ( c = 1; c < ( lrc - ulc ); c++ )      /* bottom */
    putchar ( horiz );
putchar ( br );

for ( r = 1; r < ( lrr - ulr ); r++ ) { /* left side */
    locate ( ulr + r, ulc );
    putchar ( vert );
}
for ( r = 1; r < ( lrr - ulr ); r++ ) { /* right side */
    locate ( ulr + r, lrc );
    putchar ( vert );
}
rcp ();                                 /* restore cursor */
```

# CHAPTER 4

# SYSTEMS PROGRAMMING FUNCTIONS FOR THE IBM PC AND COMPATIBLES

*O*ne of the characteristics that makes C such a powerful programming language is its ability to get down very close to machine level. C is often called a "middle-level language" because it purportedly exists somewhere between the grassroots of assembler and the sweeping breadth of the likes of PL/I and COBOL. In fact, however, C is as good at advanced calculations and data handling as any of the high-level languages. A case can thus be made that the so-called high-level languages are less capable than C, and C is better than assembler for almost any conceivable programming purpose except those requiring low-level register manipulation.

In this chapter we set out to explore some of the systems programming capabilities available in C on the IBM PC and compatible MS-DOS machines. By "systems programming" I don't mean writing a new operating system, but instead operations—many of them useful in applications programs—that interface directly with the two "doorways" to the machine level: the BIOS (Basic Input/Output System) and the DOS internal functions. Many of these operations can be done at a higher level, but at the expense of considerable overhead; see Chapter 3. The advantages of going directly to machine level are speed, efficiency, tightness of code, and absolute control. Many of these functions seem magical; screens full of data leap instantly on the display, for example, and they enable you to do windowing and other tricks possible, but difficult, in most languages.

Though C is a comprehensive language, it falls an inch short of total completeness in its inability to address specific CPU registers. This is not so much a failing of the language as a logical outgrowth of its portability; the number of registers and their names and purposes vary from one machine to another, making it impossible or at least exceedingly impractical to accommodate every possible CPU configuration within the syntax of the C language itself. Consequently, at the lowest level, it's necessary to resort to short assembly-language routines that accept variables and load them into the appropriate registers, execute an interrupt, and pass the results back to the caller.

This chapter contains two such assembly-language routines, one for calling the BIOS, the other for addressing the operating system. They are essential to the operation of every function in this chapter. They are also, regrettably, the subject of a few words of caution. Different compilers utilize different methods for calling subprograms. One might pass parameters on the stack, whereas another might pass a count of the parameters and an address where they're stored in memory. I wrote these routines for DeSmet C, and I guarantee that they work for that particular environment. They might or might not work for Lattice, Mark Williams, Whitesmith's, or whatever C product you use. It is advisable (nay, crucial) that before attempting to use these functions, you consult your compiler's manual. Most C compiler manuals contain a section entitled something on the order of "Interfacing Assembly-Language Routines" and also explain how to use the in-line assembler feature. Look also for a description of "prologue" and "epilogue" processing, which explains the compiler's conventions automatically supplied at the start and end of each C function. These discussions and a good reference on assembly-language programming [I recommend *Programming the 8086/8088,* by James W. Coffron (Berkeley, Calif.: Sybex, Inc., 1983)] should be enough to enable you to modify the bios and dosf functions to work with your compiler. All other "straight C" functions will then operate, and the magic kingdom of direct control over the machine will belong to you.

I should add, incidentally, that modification of the assembly language is only to accommodate the way your compiler works; it will not limit the portability of your programs to other MS-DOS machines, assuming that those other machines (and/or yours) are highly compatible with the IBM PC. With "sort of compatibles," such as the Texas Instruments Professional and the Tandy 2000, these functions might work, and then again, they might not. The major compatibility issue among PC clones is in the BIOS, which controls the display memory and thus the screen. I developed these functions on a Compaq Portable and tested them on an IBM PC/XT and a Zenith Z-150, and they worked flawlessly in all cases. Not having access to other, perhaps less-compatible, machines, I can't speak for the functions' success on them.

As you will see throughout, the key to passing parameters to both the bios and dosf functions is to present values in an order related directly to the four general-purpose register pairs of the 8Ø86/8Ø88 processor, which are called AX, BX, CX, and DX. Both functions load the first two parameters into the "high" and "low" (AH and AL) halves of the AX pair. Thereafter, the parameters are full 16-bit integers destined for BX, CX, and DX, which necessitates multiplying any value intended for the "high" byte by 256 to shift it to the proper position.

In addition, both functions expect the last parameter to be the address of a four-element array of integers, where the function writes the register values returned by the system interrupt and passes them back to the calling program. From there you can extract any contents that are of interest. Where a register pair holds two discrete values, you can get the upper byte through division by 256 ( upper = val / 256 ) and the lower with modulo-256 ( lower = val % 256 ).

The C functions do all this converting and extracting for you and can serve as a guide if you choose to expand this library with some of your own functions. An excellent source of information about using the BIOS and DOS functions, by the way, is *The IBM PC-DOS Handbook,* by Richard Allen King (Berkeley, Calif.: Sybex, Inc., 1983). It explains them in plain, concise English, which cannot be said of IBM's documentation.

The functions in this chapter are as follows:

### *BIOS Group*

| | |
|---|---|
| bios | Assembly-language interface to the BIOS. |
| cursize | Modifies the size and form of the cursor. |
| rd_mode | Reads the current screen mode and attributes. |
| set_mode | Sets the screen mode. |
| set_page | Sets the active display page. |
| fillscrn | Fills the selected page with a fixed character. |
| clr_scrn | Clears the selected page. |
| home | Homes the cursor without clearing the page. |
| get_curs | Gets the cursor position and size. |
| put_curs | Places the cursor. |
| clr_eol | Clears from the current cursor position to the end of the line. |

| clr_eos | Clears from the current cursor position to the end of the screen. |
|---------|---------|
| rd_char | Reads the character at the current cursor position. |
| txt_attr | Builds a text-attribute byte to govern foreground, background, and blinking. |
| put_text | Places text at a specified row/column in the selected page, with optional attributes. |
| win_up | Scrolls a text window upward. |
| win_dn | Scrolls a text window downward. |
| dot | Writes a graphics dot (pixel). |
| line | Draws a line or a rectangle. |
| circle | Draws a circle or an ellipse. |

### DOS Group

| dosf | Assembly-language interface to DOS. |
|------|---------|
| dos_ver | DOS version number. |
| mkdir | Make a subdirectory. |
| rmdir | Remove a subdirectory. |
| chdir | Change directories. |
| dskparms | Get disk parameters. |
| diskspc | Get free space on a disk (in bytes). |

# BIOS Group

## bios

## ( ah, al, bx, cx, dx, results )

**Description:**   This is written as a C function, but it consists of in-line assembly language. It accepts parameters from the calling program, places them into the CPU registers, and calls the BIOS with an interrupt. When the BIOS returns, the function stores the register contents into the results array as 16-bit integers and returns to the caller, which must then extract any values of interest from the array. Refer to the preface to this chapter.

The values that go into the registers as parameters vary with the BIOS function being called. Technical references dealing with DOS and the BIOS detail the parameters. Where a BIOS function does not expect a parametric value in a particular register or register pair, pass a 0 parameter in the corresponding position to serve as a placeholder.

**Parameters:**

ah is the BIOS function code, which will be placed into the AH register.
al is a value to be placed into the AL register.
bx is an integer to be placed into the BX register.
cx is an integer to be placed into the CX register.
dx is an integer to be placed into the DX register.
results is the name (implied address) of an array of four integers where the function will return the contents of the registers.

**Type of Value Returned:**   None (results array is loaded with the returned values of the registers following the BIOS call).

**Other Functions Called:**   None.

**Remarks:**   Note that the formal function listing itself (unlike the descriptive heading above) does not stipulate the parameters. This is because bios extracts them directly from the stack, and thus no parameter declarations are required in order to locate them. *This function is written for DeSmet C and may require revision to work with your compiler!* See the discussion at the start of this chapter for further information.

```
bios ( )              /* call BIOS for screen control */
{

    /* Parms are registers ah, al, bx, cx, dx and a pointer
       to an array of integers where 'bios' will return the
       ax - dx register values after the function executes */

    /* NOTE: inline assembly code for DeSmet C -- check your
       compiler's documentation, change calling conventions
       and inline directives if appropriate */

#asm
    mov         ah, [ bp +  4 ]
    mov         al, [ bp +  6 ]
    mov         bx, [ bp +  8 ]
    mov         cx, [ bp + 10 ]
    mov         dx, [ bp + 12 ]
    int         10h
    push        bp
    mov         bp, [ bp + 14 ]
    mov         [ bp + 0 ], ax
    mov         [ bp + 2 ], bx
    mov         [ bp + 4 ], cx
    mov         [ bp + 6 ], dx
    pop         bp
#
}
```

## cursize

## ( top, bottom )

*Description:*   A character cell on the IBM PC and compatibles is an area 14 scan lines high, ranging from the tops of tall letters such as capitals to the "tails" of descenders on such characters as g and p. These scan lines are numbered from Ø on top to 13 on the bottom. The cursor is ordinarily a double underscore at scan lines 12 and 13, but it can be modified to have other shapes. For example, when the cursor begins at Ø and ends at 13, it occupies the entire character cell as a vertical rectangle. You can start and end the cursor anywhere within this range of scan lines, so that if you start it and end it at Ø, it will be a thin *over*score (above the letters instead of below them). Similarly, it's possible to "wrap" the cursor, starting it at a line lower than it ends. If you start the cursor at 12 and end it at 1, you will get a double overscore and a double underscore with empty space between the halves of the cursor. This function allows you to vary the appearance of the cursor, and that appearance remains in effect on all display pages until the next time BIOS is called to change it to something else, or until the system is turned off. Word processors, as an example, often use this facility to create distinctive cursor shapes that indicate whether the program is in normal or insert mode.

*Parameters:*

> top is an integer from Ø through 13 that indicates the scan line of
> the cursor top.
> bottom is an integer in the range Ø–13 indicating the scan line of
> the cursor's bottom.

*Type of Value Returned:*   None.

*Other Functions Called:*   bios.

*Remarks:*   The function automatically corrects scan-line parameters that are out of range. It allocates a dummy array to satisfy the requirements of the bios function to have a place to return results, even though no results are expected from this call. This is merely to prevent undesirable side effects.

```
cursize ( top, bottom )          /* change cursor size */
int    top, bottom;
{
    int      dummy [ 4 ];

        top    = ( top    >  0 ) ? top    : 0;
        top    = ( top    < 13 ) ? top    : 13;
        bottom = ( bottom >  0 ) ? bottom : 0;
        bottom = ( bottom < 13 ) ? bottom : 13;
        bios ( 2, 0, 0, (( top * 256 ) + bottom ), 0, dummy );
}
```

## rd_mode

## ( results )

*Description:* It's necessary occasionally for a program, and often for a generalized function such as those in this chapter, to determine the characteristics of the current display. That's what this function does. It reads the mode—hence the name—and reports the mode number, the number of columns on the display, and the active page number, placing them in that order in the results array. The mode numbers are discussed in the description of set_mode, the next function in this chapter. The values returned in results enable the program to make decisions about how to proceed.

*Parameters:* results is the name (implied address) of an array of at least three integers where the function will report:

[0]   The current screen mode.
[1]   The number of columns on the screen.
[2]   The active page number.

*Type of Value Returned:* None (modifies results).

*Other Functions Called:* bios.

```
rd_mode ( ret_val )      /* read current screen mode */
int    ret_val [];
{
    int      prm [ 4 ];

        bios ( 15, 0, 0, 0, 0, prm );
        ret_val [ 0 ] = prm [ 0 ] % 256;    /* mode number    */
        ret_val [ 1 ] = prm [ 0 ] / 256;    /* cols on screen */
        ret_val [ 2 ] = prm [ 1 ] / 256;    /* active page nbr */
}
```

## set_mode

## ( mode )

*Description:*   The PC family of computers, when equipped with a color-graphics board, supports seven different screen modes indicated by a digit in the range Ø–6. The set_mode function allows you to select which mode you want for the display. The mode also governs how many pages of display memory the system has; the next function (set_page) discusses this further. The display mode indicators, number of pages, and formats are:

| Mode | Pages | Format |
|------|-------|--------|
| Ø | 8 | 40 × 25 monochrome text |
| 1 | 8 | 40 × 25 color text |
| 2 | 4 | 80 × 25 monochrome text |
| 3 | 4 | 80 × 25 color text |
| 4 | 2 | 320 × 200 monochrome graphics |
| 5 | 1 | 320 × 200 color graphics |
| 6 | 1 | 640 × 200 monochrome graphics |

*Parameters:*   mode is an integer specifying one of the display modes listed above.

*Type of Value Returned:*   None.

*Other Functions Called:*   bios.

*Remarks:*   Good style in C dictates that #define statements be used in the calling program to give these modes labels and thus avoid "magic numbers."

```
int set_mode ( mode )          /* set screen mode */
int    mode;
{
    int    dummy [ 4 ];                 /* needed only to satisfy 'bios' */

        if ( mode < 0 || mode > 6 )
            return ( 0 );               /* error */
        bios ( 0, mode, 0, 0, 0, dummy );
        return ( 1 );
}
```

## set_page

## ( page )

*Description:*   As the preceding function (set_mode) explains, different screen modes have differing numbers of pages available with the color/graphics board. This is because the board has 16K of memory, and so the memory requirements for the display modes allow, in all cases except modes 5 and 6, for more than one page to fill the 16K. The advantage of having extra pages is that, as the user looks at one display (the "active page," which is one visible on the screen), the program can be constructing the next display behind the scenes in an inactive page. This function brings an inactive page into view, or in other words makes it active, after it has been built and the user is ready to move onward.

*Parameters:*   page is an integer specifying a valid page number for the current display mode.

*Type of Value Returned:*   Integer: $\emptyset$ = unsuccessful (invalid page number); 1 = successful.

*Other Functions Called:*   bios.

*Remarks:*   The number of pages available under each mode is listed under set_mode above. Pages are numbered $\emptyset$ through one less than the number available; for example, mode 2 (80 × 25 monochrome text) has four pages, so the page numbers are $\emptyset$–3. The default for the IBM PC with a color-graphics card is mode 2, page $\emptyset$, and for the IBM PC*jr*, mode $\emptyset$, page $\emptyset$.

```
int set_page ( page )    /* set active page */
int    page;
{
    int    tmp [ 4 ];

        rd_mode ( tmp );
        if ( tmp [ 0 ] == 7 )
            return ( 0 );       /* page always 0 if monochrome display */
        if ( page > 7 )
            return ( 0 );                                       /* error */
        if ( tmp [ 0 ] > 1 && page > 3 )
            return ( 0 );                                       /* error */
        if ( tmp [ 0 ] == 4 && page > 1 )
            return ( 0 );
        if ( tmp [ 0 ] > 4 && page > 0 )
            return ( 0 );
        bios ( 5, page, 0, 0, 0, tmp );
        return ( 1 );                                 /* normal exit */
}
```

## fillscrn

## ( page, code )

*Description:*   This function fills the entire display page with any character you choose. It can be used, for example, to clear the screen by filling it with space characters (although the next function is specifically written to do this.). It's rather a simpleminded function in that no color attributes are allowed. Instead, it operates in normal monochrome text mode, adjusting itself automatically to 40- or 80-column output. It is an extremely fast function, filling the screen instantly. Use it for creating shaded backgrounds and other special effects.

*Parameters:*

page is a valid page number for the current mode.
code is an integer from 0–255 that specifies an ASCII character by its decimal value. This value is the character that will fill the entire page.

*Type of Value Returned:*   Integer: 0 = invalid page number; 1 = successful completion.

*Other Functions Called:*   rd_mode, home, bios.

```
int fillscrn ( page, chnbr )        /* fill screen with char # */
int page, chnbr;
{
    int     nch, tmp [ 4 ];

        rd_mode ( tmp );
        nch = tmp [ 1 ] * 25;       /* nbr chars on screen */
        if ( !home ( page ))
            return ( 0 );
        bios ( 10, chnbr, page * 256, nch, 0, tmp );
        return ( 1 );
}
```

## clr__scrn

## ( page )

*Description:* This function, as its name suggests, clears the screen by filling it with space characters. Actually, it clears the selected page, which might or might not be the active page at the moment. Thus, you can use it to clear a page "behind the scenes" in preparation for building a new screen image while the user stares at the active page on the display. It is a very simple subprogram in that it merely calls upon fillscrn to write spaces. It works at astonishing speed.

*Parameters:* page is an integer specifying a valid page for the current display mode.

*Type of Value Returned:* Integer: Ø = invalid page; 1 = success.

*Other Functions Called:* fillscrn.

---

```
clr_scrn ( page )              /* clear screen */
int     page;
{
    int      rc;

        rc = fillscrn ( page, 32 );
        return ( rc );
}
```

---

## home

**( page )**

*Description:*   This function homes (places the cursor in the upper left corner of) the selected display page. Unlike some renditions of a generalized home function, it does *not* clear the page, but instead merely places the cursor.

*Parameters:*   page is a valid page number for the current mode.

*Type of Value Returned:*   Integer: Ø = invalid page; 1 = success.

*Other Functions Called:*   rd_mode, bios.

```
int home ( page )                    /* home cursor in sel page */
int     page;
{
    int     tmp [ 4 ];

        rd_mode ( tmp );
        if ( page > 7 )
            return ( 0 );
        if ( tmp [ 0 ] > 1 && page > 3 )
            return ( 0 );
        if ( tmp [ 0 ] == 4 && page > 1 )
            return ( 0 );
        if ( tmp [ 0 ] > 4 && page > 0 )
            return ( 0 );
        bios ( 2, 0, ( page * 256 ), 0, 0, tmp );
        return ( 1 );
}
```

## get_curs

## ( page, results )

*Description:*   This function is a "double whammy"; it determines the position of the cursor in the selected page and also the starting and ending lines of the cursor's configuration. The cursor position will vary with the display page selected, but the cursor shape is consistent throughout all pages. The function returns its information in the results array as follows:

[Ø]     Cursor row
[1]     Cursor column
[2]     Starting scan line of cursor
[3]     Ending scan line of cursor

*Parameters:*

page is a valid page number for the current mode.
results is the name (implied address) of an array of four integers where the function will return results as described above.

*Type of Value Returned:*   Integer: Ø = invalid page; 1 = success.

*Other Functions Called:*   rd_mode, bios.

```c
int get_curs ( page, xy )      /* get current cursor position */
int   page, xy [];
{
    int    tmp [ 4 ];

        rd_mode ( tmp );
        if ( page > 7 )
            return ( 0 );
        if ( tmp [ 0 ] > 1 && page > 3 )
            return ( 0 );
        if ( tmp [ 0 ] == 4 && page > 1 )
            return ( 0 );
        if ( tmp [ 0 ] > 4 && page > 0 )
            return ( 0 );
        bios ( 3, 0, ( page * 256 ), 0, 0, tmp );
        xy [ 0 ] = tmp [ 3 ] / 256;          /* row      */
        xy [ 1 ] = tmp [ 3 ] % 256;          /* col      */
        xy [ 2 ] = tmp [ 2 ] / 256;       /* curs start */
        xy [ 3 ] = tmp [ 2 ] % 256;       /* curs end   */
        return ( 1 );
}
```

## put__curs

### ( page, row, col )

***Description:*** The keystone of attractive, formatted displays, this function places the cursor at the specified row and column of the selected page. Like the other page-oriented functions, this one can work on an inactive page.

***Parameters:***

page is an integer expressing a valid page number for the current mode.

row is the row number (∅ is the top row).

col is the column number (∅ is the leftmost column).

***Type of Value Returned:*** Integer: ∅ = invalid page; 1 = success.

***Other Functions Called:*** rd__mode, bios.

***Remarks:*** Row numbers are ∅−24, column numbers ∅−39 in 40-column modes and ∅−79 on 80-column screens.

```
int put_curs ( page, row, col )      /* place cursor */
int   page, row, col;
{
    int    tmp [ 4 ];

        rd_mode ( tmp );
        if ( page > 7 )
            return ( 0 );
        if ( tmp [ 0 ] > 1 && page > 3 )
            return ( 0 );
        if ( tmp [ 0 ] == 4 && page > 1 )
            return ( 0 );
        if ( tmp [ 0 ] > 4 && page > 0 )
            return ( 0 );
        if ( col > tmp [ 1 ] )
            return ( 0 );
        if ( row > 24 )
            return ( 0 );
        bios ( 2, 0, ( page * 256 ), 0, (( row * 256 ) + col ), tmp );
        return ( 1 );
}
```

## clr__eol

## ( page )

*Description:*   Unscrambling the somewhat cryptic name of this function reveals its purpose: "clear to end of line." It proceeds from the
cursor position on the selected page and fills the balance of the line (to
the rightmost column inclusive) with spaces. It has many uses. One is
to wipe away erroneous input keyed by a user, so that he or she has an
empty area in which to retype the entry.

*Parameters:*   page is a valid page number for the current mode.

*Type of Value Returned:*   Integer: $\emptyset$ = invalid page; 1 = success.

*Other Functions Called:*   rd__mode, get__curs, bios.

```
int clr_eol ( page )        /* clear to end of line from
                                current cursor position  */
int  page;
{
    int    tmp [ 4 ], nc;

        rd_mode ( tmp );
        nc = tmp [ 1 ];
        if ( !get_curs ( page, tmp ))
            return ( 0 );
        nc -= tmp [ 1 ];
        bios ( 10, 32, ( page * 256 ), nc, 0, tmp );
        return ( 1 );
}
```

## clr__eos

## ( page )

***Description:*** This function is almost identical to the preceding one (clr__eol), except that it clears the selected page from the current cursor position to the end of the screen. Anything to the left of and above the cursor remains; everything else goes. It's useful in situations where you want to leave a fixed screen heading and wipe out the variable format underneath in preparation for building a new screen image.

***Parameters:*** page is a valid page number for the current mode.

***Type of Value Returned:*** Integer: 0 = invalid page; 1 = success.

***Other Functions Called:*** rd__mode, get__curs, bios.

```
int clr_eos ( page )        /* clear to end of screen from
                                  current cursor position  */
int  page;
{
    int    tmp [ 4 ], nc;

        rd_mode ( tmp );
        nc = tmp [ 1 ];
        if ( !get_curs ( page, tmp ))
            return ( 0 );
        nc *= ( 24 - tmp [ 0 ] + 1 );
        nc -= tmp [ 1 ];
        bios ( 10, 32, ( page * 256 ), nc, 0, tmp );
        return ( 1 );
}
```

## rd_char

## ( page, &attribute )

*Description:*   This function reads the character at the current cursor position within the selected page and returns it directly as a value of type char. In addition, it indirectly returns the attribute byte for the character by loading it into the attribute parameter. Attribute bytes are discussed in detail in the headnotes for the next function (txt_attr). In order for the attribute byte to be accessible to the calling program, you must pass an address parameter for attribute, hence the "&" operator preceding the parameter name (the name of an array of integer will also suffice, in which case rd_char returns the attribute in element Ø of the array). Though seldom used, this function can be invaluable in applications where the user is encouraged to use the cursor-arrow keys in making menu selections.

*Parameters:*

   page is a valid page number for the current mode.
   &attribute is the address of an integer variable in which the function returns the character's attribute byte.

*Type of Value Returned:*   Character directly, attribute byte indirectly.

*Other Functions Called:*   bios.

*Remarks:*   Though actually a character (or byte) value, attribute is treated as an integer by the function.

```
char rd_char ( page, attrib )      /* read char and attrib at
                                        current cursor position */
int    page, attrib;
{
    char     c;
    int      tmp [ 4 ];

        attrib = 0;
        if ( page > 7 )
            return ( 0 );
        if ( tmp [ 0 ] > 1 && page > 3 )
            return ( 0 );
        if ( tmp [ 0 ] == 4 && page > 1 )
            return ( 0 );
        if ( tmp [ 0 ] > 4 && page > 0 )
            return ( 0 );
        bios ( 8, 0, ( page * 256 ), 0, 0, tmp );
        attrib = tmp [ 1 ];        /* attribute byte */
        return ( tmp [ 0 ] );          /* character */
}
```

## txt__attr

## ( foreground, background, blink )

*Description:*   With the color-graphics board, the IBM PC and compatibles are capable of producing text in any of 16 colors against a background of any of eight colors, with the characters themselves (but not the background) steady or blinking. To accomplish the requisite combination of foreground, background, and blinking, it's necessary to furnish the BIOS with an attribute byte. The txt__attr function builds the necessary attribute byte and returns it directly as a value of type char. The blink parameter is 1 if you want the text to blink and Ø if you don't. As to the colors and their applicability, the following numbers should be passed in the foreground and background parameters (see remarks for set__mode):

| f/g | b/g | Number | Color |
| --- | --- | --- | --- |
| X | X | Ø | Black |
| X | X | 1 | Blue |
| X | X | 2 | Green |
| X | X | 3 | Cyan |
| X | X | 4 | Red |
| X | X | 5 | Magenta |
| X | X | 6 | Brown |
| X | X | 7 | Light gray |
| X |   | 8 | Dark gray |
| X |   | 9 | Light blue |
| X |   | 10 | Light green |
| X |   | 11 | Light cyan |
| X |   | 12 | Light red |
| X |   | 13 | Light magenta |
| X |   | 14 | Yellow |
| X |   | 15 | White |

   When txt__attr completes, it returns a byte whose bits are set to communicate your parameters to the BIOS, so that text produced with this attribute byte (as in put__text in the following section) has the attributes your program has established.

***Parameters:***

> foreground is an integer in the range 0–15 selected from the preceding table.
>
> background is an integer in the range 0–7 selected from the preceding table.
>
> blink is 0 if you don't want the text to blink and 1 if you do (other values will cause unpredictable results).

***Type of Value Returned:*** char.

***Other Functions Called:*** None.

```c
char txt_attr ( fg, bg, blink )      /* build text attribute byte */
int  fg, bg, blink;
{
    char    f, b, bl;

        bl = blink * 128;
        b  = bg * 16;
        f  = fg & 15;
        return ( bl | b | f );
}
```

## put_text

**( page, row, col, attribute, text )**

*Description:*   This function draws together several functions already presented in this chapter. It allows you to write a string of text wherever you want within a selected page, using either a predefined attribute (created by txt_attr preceding) or the default light-on-black monochrome attribute. For example, if you want to place the line "This is the text" on page 1, row 14, column 27, in normal mode, code the call with

> if ( !put_text ( 1, 14, 27, Ø, "This is the text" )) [ error action ]

*Parameters:*

> page is a valid page number for the current mode.
> row is an integer in the range Ø–24.
> col is an integer in the range Ø–39 for 40-column displays or Ø–79 for 80-column.
> attribute is a byte of type char furnishing the text attributes in accordance with the discussion under the heading txt_attr above, or Ø if you want to use the default (light-on-black) attribute. The entire output of text will conform to this attribute.
> text is either the name of a character array or a literal string that is to be output by the function.

*Type of Value Returned:*   Integer: Ø = invalid page or invalid column; 1 = success.

*Other Functions Called:*   put_curs, bios.

```
int put_text ( page, row, col, attrib, text )    /* writes a line
                                     of text at specified location */
int     page, row, col;
char    attrib, text [];
{
    int     tmp [ 4 ], p = 0;
    char    ch;

        if ( attrib == 0 )
            attrib = 15;
        while ( ch = text [ p++ ] ) {
            if ( !put_curs ( page, row, col++ ))
                return ( 0 );
            bios ( 9, ch, ( page * 256 ) + attrib, 1, 0, tmp );
        }
```

## ( page, lines, ulx, uly, lrx, lry, attribute )

***Description:*** Writing a true windowing application is a daunting task to be undertaken only by the foolish and otherwise overconfident. Nevertheless, it is possible and perhaps easier than one might think to create text windows—one for status messages, another for input, still another for normal output—that exist more or less independently of each other on the same screen. It is not our purpose here (nor is it practical) to develop a comprehensive library of windowing utilities. On the other hand, there are two important and universally applicable windowing operations that do belong here.

The first of these is upward scrolling of a text window. A window in general is any area on the screen that you set aside for a specific purpose. You can outline the window if you wish; the line function presented below serves this purpose admirably. It's not necessary to border the window, however. Just because you arbitrarily select an area (indicated by the coordinates of its upper left and lower right corners) as a window does not mean the system recognizes it as such. It's your responsibility to ensure that text within the window doesn't slop outside. How you control that is up to you.

What this function does is to scroll the text within a designated area upward, in the same manner that the entire display scrolls in normal, nonwindowed operation. The difference is that with the win__up function, only the text within the window scrolls. Any text at the top of the window vanishes, and space opens at the bottom of the window. Displays to the right and left of the window remain unchanged; the function affects only text inside the rectangular area indicated by the upper left and lower right coordinates.

The win__up function does more than normal full-screen scrolling. You can use it to scroll a window on an inactive page, and you can scroll more than one line if you wish. Also, you can pass an attribute byte that governs the text characteristics of the new lines coming onto the bottom of the window. This is useful, for example, in establishing a unique background color for the window to set it apart visually from the rest of the display, and/or for displaying text within the window in a distinctive color. Thus, while this is not the only windowing function anybody will ever need, it is an important and powerful utility for those who toil in the vineyards of user-friendliness.

*Parameters:*

> page is a valid page for the current mode, where the window scroll will occur.
>
> lines is an integer specifying how many rows of the window are to be scrolled.
>
> ulx, uly are the row and column coordinates of the upper left corner of the window.
>
> lrx, lry are the row and column coordinates of the lower left corner of the window.
>
> attribute is a byte of type char specifying the attributes of the text to appear in the new rows of the window. If you pass Ø as an attribute, the function will set the default text attribute (light text on a black background).

*Type of Value Returned:*   Integer: Ø = invalid page or window outside the bounds of the display; 1 = success.

*Other Functions Called:*   rd___mode, bios.

```
int win_up ( page, lines, ulx, uly, lrx, lry, attrib )
int   page, ulx, uly, lrx, lry;          /* scroll window up */
char  attrib;
{
    int      tmp [ 4 ];

        rd_mode ( tmp );
        if ( page > 7 )
            return ( 0 );
        if ( tmp [ 0 ] > 1 && page > 3 )
            return ( 0 );
        if ( tmp [ 0 ] == 4 && page > 1 )
            return ( 0 );
        if ( tmp [ 0 ] > 4 && page > 0 )
            return ( 0 );
        if ( uly > tmp [ 1 ] || lry > tmp [ 1 ] )
            return ( 0 );
        if ( attrib == 0 )
            attrib = 15;
        bios ( 6, lines, ( attrib * 256 ), ( ulx * 256 ) + uly,
               ( lrx * 256 ) + lry, tmp );
        return ( 1 );
}
```

**win__dn**

## ( page, lines, ulx, uly, lrx, lry, attribute )

*Description:* This function is very similar to the last one. The only difference is that its effect is the exact opposite; it scrolls *downward* within a window defined by its northwest and southeast corners. Downward scrolling is common in word processors, data bases, program-preparation editors, and spreadsheets, all of which regard the display (or a portion of it) as a movable window giving a view of part of the information in memory.

*Parameters:*

> page is a valid page for the current mode, where the window scroll will occur.
>
> lines is an integer specifying how many rows of the window are to be scrolled.
>
> ulx, uly are the row and column coordinates of the upper left corner of the window.
>
> lrx, lry are the row and column coordinates of the lower left corner of the window.
>
> attribute is a byte of type char specifying the attributes of the text to appear in the new rows of the window. If you pass Ø as an attribute, the function will set the default text attribute (light text on a black background).

*Type of Value Returned:* Integer: Ø = invalid page or window outside the bounds of the display; 1 = success.

*Other Functions Called:* rd__mode, bios.

```c
int win_dn ( page, lines, ulx, uly, lrx, lry, attrib )
int   page, ulx, uly, lrx, lry;          /* scroll window down */
char  attrib;
{
    int     tmp [ 4 ];

        rd_mode ( tmp );
        if ( page > 7 )
            return ( 0 );
        if ( tmp [ 0 ] > 1 && page > 3 )
            return ( 0 );
        if ( tmp [ 0 ] == 4 && page > 1 )
            return ( 0 );
        if ( tmp [ 0 ] > 4 && page > 0 )
            return ( 0 );
        if ( uly > tmp [ 1 ] || lry > tmp [ 1 ] )
            return ( 0 );
        if ( attrib == 0 )
            attrib = 15;
        bios ( 7, lines, ( attrib * 256 ), ( ulx * 256 ) + uly,
                ( lrx * 256 ) + lry, tmp );
        return ( 1 );
}
```

## dot

## ( x, y, color )

*Description:* The ability to place a dot (or *pixel*) is the basis of all computer graphics, inasmuch as images are created by orderly groupings of dots on the screen. The dot function allows you to write a pixel anywhere on the graphics screens (modes 4, 5, and 6). For that matter, it also permits you to write dots off the viewing area; since they can't be seen, nothing actually happens, but the function "pretends" that it has done the program's bidding, and in the process protects adjacent areas from corruption by invalid coordinates and prevents system crashes.

Because of these safeguards, the function runs somewhat slower than it could. If you can absolutely guarantee that your programs will never attempt to address graphics coordinates outside the viewing area, go ahead and remove the first four if statements to gain a small speed advantage. My own view is that, although the function isn't lightning fast like the others given above, it's better to be safe than sorry; bizarre and disgraceful things can happen to computers when unexpected values cause the software to rampage about in places where it doesn't belong.

The dot function also contains a couple of other ounces of prevention. The color attribute refers to the four colors of the active (in this case, default) palette, which are designated by the digits Ø–3 in mode 5 (color graphics). In modes 4 and 6, the only "colors" you get are background (Ø) and foreground (1). Thus, if you specify an out-of-range color for the dot, the function will replace it with the default foreground color (1 in modes 4 and 6, 3 in mode 5).

*Parameters:*

> x and y are integers giving the dot's position. In all modes, y is visible in the range Ø–199. In modes 4 and 5, x is visible in the range Ø–319, and in mode 6 it's visible in the range Ø–639.
> color is an integer specifying the color of the dot. See the last paragraph under Description above for further discussion.

*Type of Value Returned:* None.

*Other Functions Called:* rd_mode, bios.

*Remarks:* Note that this function only works on the active page.

```
dot ( x, y, color )                  /* write dot in graphics mode */
int    x, y, color;
{
    int      tmp [ 4 ];

        rd_mode ( tmp );
        if ( tmp [ 0 ] < 4 )
            return;             /* if not in graphics mode */
        if ( y < 0 || y > 199 || x < 0 )
            return;                /* off the screen – no action */
        if ( tmp [ 0 ] < 6 && x > 319 )
            return;
        if ( tmp [ 0 ] == 6 && x > 639 )
            return;
        if ( color < 0 || color > 3 )
            color = 3;           /* default color on error */
        if ( tmp [ 0 ] == 6 || color > 1 )
            color = 1;
        bios ( 12, color, 0, x, y, tmp );
}
```

**line**

# ( x1, y1, x2, y2, color, box )

**Description:**   The line function is similar to the LINE instruction in BASIC, except that it goes one better. It is modeled on the LINE statement available in PC*jr* BASIC, which is superior to the one on the larger IBM PC and compatibles. This function draws a line between two points designated by x1, y1, and x2, y2 (using graphics coordinates), but it can also draw a rectangle defined by the coordinates of two opposite corners. The line or box can be in any valid color for the mode, since it uses the dot function discussed above to construct the actual image. This also means that the end points of the line or box can be off the screen's viewing area.

The function draws a rectangle when the box parameter has a value of 1, and a line when the parameter is anything else: nominally Ø. You can specify the coordinates in any order, either as end points for a line or as opposing corners of a rectangle (NW-SE or NE-SW). A certain amount of sorting occurs to ensure that the function always works first left-to-right, then higher-to-lower, no matter what the order of the co-ordinates passed as parameters.

Though long, this is an excellent general-purpose graphics function. Because of the safeguards contained by it and also by dot, it is not par-ticularly fast, but it is serviceable, and in any event it's faster than its corresponding instruction in BASIC.

**Parameters:**

   x1, y1 are the integral graphics coordinates for one end point of a
      line or for one corner of a rectangle.
   x2, y2 are the graphics coordinates for the other end point of the
      line or the opposite corner of the rectangle.
   color is an integer specifying a valid color for the current mode (see
      dot for further discussion).
   box is integer 1 for a rectangle and any other integer (nominally Ø)
      for a line.

**Type of Value Returned:**   None.

**Other Functions Called:**   slope, dot.

```
line ( x1, y1, x2, y2, color, box )    /* line or rectangle */
int    x1, y1, x2, y2, color, box;
{
    int     x, y;
    double  slope (), dx1, dy1, dx2, dy2, dx, dy, sl;

        if ( box > 1 )
            box = 0;    /* can only be 0 or 1 */
        switch ( box ) {
            case 1:             /* draw rectangle */
                it ( x2 < x1 ) {
                    x  = x1;
                    x1 = x2;
                    x2 = x;
                }
                if ( y2 < y1 ) {
                    y  = y1;
                    y1 = y2;
                    y2 = y;
                }
                for ( x = x1; x <= x2; x++ ) {
                    dot ( x, y1, color );
                    dot ( x, y2, color );
                }
                for ( y = y1; y <= y2; y++ ) {
                    dot ( x1, y, color );
                    dot ( x2, y, color );
                }
                break;
            case 0:          /* draw line */
                if ( x1 == x2 ) {        /* vertical */
                    if ( y2 < y1 ) {
                        y  = y1;
                        y1 = y2;
                        y2 = y;
                    }
                    for ( y = y1; y <= y2; y++ )
                        dot ( x1, y, color );
                    break;
                }
                if ( y1 == y2 ) {        /* horizontal */
                    if ( x2 < x1 ) {
                        x  = x1;
                        x1 = x2;
                        x2 = x;
                    }
                    for ( x = x1; x <= x2; x++ )
                        dot ( x, y1, color );
                    break;
                }
```

```
/* diagonal routines follow */
/* plots along the longer of the x or y axis to make solid line */

          if ( abs ( x1 - x2 ) > abs ( y1, y2 )) {
              if ( x2 < x1 ) {            /* x axis is longer */
                  x  = x1;    y  = y1;
                  x1 = x2;    y1 = y2;
                  x2 = x;     y2 = y;
              }
              dx1 = x1;    dy1 = y1;
              dx2 = x2;    dy2 = y2;
              dy  = dy1;
              sl = slope ( dx1, dy1, dx2, dy2 );
              for ( x = x1; x <= x2; x++ ) {
                  y = dy;
                  dot ( x, y, color );
                  dy += sl;
              }
              break;
          }
          if ( y1 > y2 ) {        /* y axis is longer */
              x  = x1;    y  = y1;
              x1 = x2;    y1 = y2;
              x2 = x;     y2 = y;
          }
          dx1 = x1;    dy1 = y1;
          dx2 = x2;    dy2 = y2;
          dx  = dx1;
          sl  = 1 / slope ( dx1, dy1, dx2, dy2 );
          for ( y = y1; y <= y2; y++ ) {
              x = dx;
              dot ( x, y, color );
              dx += sl;
          }
          break;

    }
}
```

## circle

## ( cx, cy, radius, color, aspect )

*Description:*   This function and the last one (line) are somewhat afield from the topic of systems programming, but they demonstrate the other BIOS subprograms in a useful and meaningful way. The circle function, as you might have guessed, draws a circle on a graphics screen. It also draws ellipses—circles elongated either vertically or horizontally—by altering the aspect parameter. For those not familiar with graphics programaming, some explanation of aspect ratio is in order.

Nearly all computer displays (Apple's Macintosh being perhaps the sole exception) suffer from a condition known as orthogonal distortion. In general, computer screens have different units of measurement vertically and horizontally; five units vertically is the same physical distance as six units horizontally. The consequence as regards circles is that, without adjusting for this distortion, any circle you draw will end up being an ellipse—in this case, longer vertically than it is horizontally, by a factor of 6-to-5. In high-resolution graphics (mode 6) the distortion is twice as bad, or 5/12. The circle function automatically makes the adjustment appropriate for the current mode, so that if you furnish as aspect parameter of 1.Ø, the resulting circle will end up being as perfectly round as your display can accommodate.

But let's suppose that you actually want to draw an ellipse, and that you want it to be 80 percent as high as it is wide. You can do this by passing an aspect parameter of Ø.8. Or if you want it to be 50 percent higher than its width, you can pass aspect as 1.5. The subprogram will make the necessary adjustments to accomplish any aspect ratio of height to width that you specify. In other words, aspect governs the height of the result relative to its width. In all cases, the radius parameter specifies the radius (distance from center points cx and cy to the perimeter) along the horizontal axis, and aspect modifies the distance from center to top and bottom as a percentage of the horizontal.

This function is useful and reasonably "slick" for simple circle making. It will place a circle or ellipse anywhere on the screen with any radius you specify, and since it uses the dot function to create the image, part of the circle can lie outside the display boundaries without causing nasty side effects. On the other hand, it is limited in its usefulness for making pie charts, arcs, and other such modified circles.

*Parameters:*

cx and cy are integers specifying the center coordinates of the circle.

radius is an integer giving the *horizontal* radius of the figure in units corresponding to the horizontal *x* coordinates of the current display mode (320 for modes 4 and 5, 640 for mode 6).

color is a valid color code for the current mode.

aspect is a double, giving the ratio of height to width (where 1.0 is a perfect circle).

*Type of Value Returned:* None.

*Other Functions Called:* rd_mode, dot, plus standard library.

```
circle ( cx, cy, radius, color, aspect )
int      cx, cy, radius, color;
double   aspect;
{
    int      angle, x, y, tmp [ 4 ];
    double   sin (), cos (), ar, rad, f = 3.14159 / 180.0;

        rd_mode ( tmp );
        if ( tmp [ 0 ] < 4 )
            return;              /* not in graphics mode */
        ar = ( tmp [ 0 ] < 6 ) ? ( 5.0 / 6.0 ) : ( 5.0 / 12.0 );
        ar *= aspect;
        for ( angle = 0; angle < 91; angle++ ) {
            rad = (( double ) ( angle ) * f );
            x = ( int ) ( cos ( rad ) * radius );
            y = ( int ) ( sin ( rad ) * radius * ar );
            dot ( cx + x, cy + y, color );
            dot ( cx - x, cy + y, color );
            dot ( cx + x, cy - y, color );
            dot ( cx - x, cy - y, color );
        }
}
```

# DOS Group

The DOS functions given here are much fewer than the BIOS group. This is not because DOS does less for you, but because the C language contains most standard-library facilities for accomplishing the things that programmers often need to do. This is one of the major advantages of C; it is portable to the extent that common operating-system utilities are embedded within the standard library, no matter what environment you utilize.

Thus, the functions that we present here are those unique to the PC-DOS/MS-DOS operating system, and usually missing from C products. You may, of course, expand this library to suit yourself. The dosf function is generalized to the same degree as bios earlier, and the only significant difference in the two is the interrupt they generate. Consequently, you are at liberty to expand upon this library as your programming needs dictate. Be aware, however, that your additional functions may conflict—or at best duplicate—those already available under the compiler's standard library.

## dosf

# ( function, al, bx, cx, dx, results )

***Description:***   This function is very similar to bios presented some pages earlier. The difference is that it generates an interrupt to the DOS operating system, rather than to the BIOS. It is thus suitable chiefly for file management and other things for which the operating system is responsible, rather than for screen control.

In general, every program call to the operating system occurs through interrupt 21H (decimal 33), and the number of the specific DOS function you want to perform is loaded into register AH. DOS then returns its results in registers AX–DX, which are four 16-bit registers that your program must interpret in ways associated with the call. Sometimes other parameters are required for the call in registers AL, BX, CX, and DX; in those cases, it's necessary to pass the appropriate values in positional parameters. When a register or register pair does not convey a value, pass Ø as the value of its parameter.

With this function, it is *always* mandatory to pass the name (implied address) of an array of four integers so that the dosf function will have a place in which to return the contents of the CPU registers. The functions that follow dosf serve as examples showing how to accomplish this, and the interpretation of register contents.

***Parameters:***

> function is an integer indicating the DOS function you want to perform.
>
> ah is a supplementary integer value to be placed into the AH register as required by the function being called.
>
> bx, cx, and dx are other 16-bit (integer) values to be placed in the respective registers as information required by the call being made.
>
> results is the name (implied address) of an array of four integers where the function will return the contents of the registers.

***Type of Value Returned:***   None (returned indirectly in results, in the order: [Ø] AX, [1] BX, [2] CS, and [3] DX.

***Other Functions Called:***   None.

***Remarks:***   The same cautions apply here as for bios regarding calling conventions and in-line assembly.

```
dosf ( )                    /* call PC-DOS or MS-DOS for function */
{
    /* Parms are registers ah, al, bx, cx, dx and a pointer
       to an array of integers where DOS will return the
       ax - dx register values after the function executes */

    /* NOTE: inline assembly code for DeSmet C -- check your
       compiler's documentation, change calling conventions
       and inline directives if appropriate */

#asm
    mov         ah, [ bp +  4 ]
    mov         al, [ bp +  6 ]
    mov         bx, [ bp +  8 ]
    mov         cx, [ bp + 10 ]
    mov         dx, [ bp + 12 ]
    int         21h
    push        bp
    mov         bp, [ bp + 14 ]
    mov         [ bp + 0 ], ax
    mov         [ bp + 2 ], bx
    mov         [ bp + 4 ], cx
    mov         [ bp + 6 ], dx
    pop         bp
#
}
```

## dos_ver

## ( results )

*Description:*   This function returns the PC-DOS/MS-DOS version number under which the program is operating. The rationale, in C notation, is that:

```
if ( VERSION > 1 )
    [ DOS 2.x is active ]
else
    [ DOS 1.x is active ]
```

It is possible, of course, to expand this further with versions 3.0 and later, and to govern the program's expectations of DOS accordingly. As of this writing, DOS 3.x is too new for me to suggest what those "expectations" might be, but the differences between 1.x and 2.x are significant and well-established; one could not, for example, expect 1.x to support subdirectories, whereas that's entirely reasonable under 2.x.

The dos_ver function returns the major version level in results [0] and the minor (revision) level in results [1]. For example, if your program is operating under DOS 2.1 and you call this function, the results array will afterward contain [0] = 2 and [1] = 1.

*Parameters:*   results is the name (implied address) of an array of at least two integers where the function will return the version's major and minor levels as discussed above.

*Type of Value Returned:*   None (see Description above).

*Other Functions Called:*   dosf.

```
dos_ver ( results )         /* get DOS version number */
int  results [];
{
    int     tmp [ 4 ];

        dosf ( 48, 0, 0, 0, 0, tmp );
        results [ 0 ] = tmp [ 0 ] % 256;    /* major version */
        results [ 1 ] = tmp [ 0 ] / 256;    /* minor version */
}
```

## mkdir

## ( pathname )

*Description:* This function does the same thing as the DOS command MKDIR, except that it does it from within a program. The `pathname` parameter can be either a literal or a pointer to an array of characters containing the disk drive and the name of the subdirectory to be created. For example, to create a new subdirectory called TESTDIR on the C drive, the function call is

```
mkdir ( "C:\TESTDIR" );
```

The use of backslash corresponds to DOS usage.

In actual practice, calls to `mkdir` should check its return code. The function always returns an integer that corresponds to the standard DOS 2+ function call error indicators. The range of these codes is 1–18. When `mkdir` returns a value outside this range, it completed successfully. For the meanings of valid error codes 1–18, see Chapter 5 ("DOS Interrupts and Function Calls") of the PC-DOS/MS-DOS manual. In testing, the function always returned 254 as an "okay" return code, but whether this is unvaryingly so is not clear. It would be safer to write the return-code check as

```
if ( mkdir ( path ) <= 18 )
      [ an error occurred ]
else
      [ completed okay ]
```

*Parameters:* `pathname` is a literal or the name of a character array containing the drive designator and the new subdirectory name.

*Type of Value Returned:* Integer. See Description above.

*Other Functions Called:* dosf.

```c
int mkdir ( pathname )       /* make directory */
char     pathname [];
{
    int    tmp [ 4 ];

        dosf ( 57, 0, 0, 0, pathname, tmp );
        return ( tmp [ 0 ] );
}
```

## rmdir

## ( pathname )

*Description:*   Like mkdir in the preceding section, this function takes its name from the equivalent DOS command. It removes a subdirectory from the drive specified in pathname, provided that the subdirectory is empty (doesn't point to any files). This is a restriction imposed by DOS itself as a safeguard against blowing away files by inadvertently killing their directory.

   The function returns an integer that is identical in significance to the return codes emanating from mkdir. See the discussion above for more information. When successful, it returns an integer outside the error code range 1–18.

*Parameters:*   pathname is a literal or the name of a character array containing the drive designator and the new subdirectory name.

*Type of Value Returned:*   Integer. See Description above.

*Other Functions Called:*   dosf.

```
int rmdir ( pathname )     /* remove directory */
char    pathname [];
{
    int     tmp [ 4 ];

        dosf ( 58, 0, 0, 0, pathname, tmp );
        return ( tmp [ 0 ] );
}
```

## chdir

### ( pathname )

*Description:*   This is the last of the subdirectory functions whose names ape the DOS commands. The chdir function logs the system onto the drive and subdirectory given by the pathname. Like the two preceding functions, it returns an integer which, when in the range 1–18, indicates an error, and otherwise means the function completed successfully.

*Parameters:*   pathname is a literal or the name of a character array containing the drive designator and the new subdirectory name.

*Type of Value Returned:*   Integer. See Description above.

*Other Functions Called:*   dosf.

```
int chdir ( pathname )    /* change directory */
char    pathname [];
{
    int    tmp [ 4 ];

        dosf ( 59, 0, 0, 0, pathname, tmp );
        return ( tmp [ 0 ] );
}
```

## dskparms

## ( drive, parm )

*Description:* In systems programming, and in applications as well, it's sometimes necessary to find out what sort of characteristics a disk has. That way you can have the program modify its behavior to suit the environment. The dskparms function allows you to query the drive about the disk it contains. It works equally well for floppy, hard, or semiconductor disks, returning the results in the parm array.

The returned information is essentially everything you'd ever want to know about a disk. From it you can derive specific information you need to know by mathematical processes. The diskspc function in the following section demonstrates one such calculation.

*Parameters:*

drive is an integer (*not* a letter!), in which Ø indicates the default drive, 1 = A, 2 = B, etc.

parm is an array of four integers in which the function returns information about the disk as follows:

parm [ Ø ] = Sectors per cluster (see Remarks)
parm [ 1 ] = Number of free clusters
parm [ 2 ] = Bytes per sector
parm [ 3 ] = Total clusters on the drive

*Type of Value Returned:* None directly (indirectly in parm).

*Other Functions Called:* dosf.

*Remarks:* Note the spelling of this function's name: no "i" where you might expect one. This is due to the 8-character limit on DOS filenames and also, in many cases, on C function names.

When parm [ Ø ] contains the value 65535 (hex FFFF), it means that the disk drive you specified does not exist. In that case, the rest of the parm array contains garbage.

```
dskparms ( drive, parm )      /* get disk parameters (DOS 2+) */
int    drive, parm [];
{
    dosf ( 54, 0, 0, 0, drive, parm );
}
```

## diskspc

## ( drive )

*Description:*   Before creating a new file and writing tons of data to it, it's not a bad idea to find out if there's enough space on the disk to hold it all. Programs seldom know in advance how much data they're going to generate, but if you as the programmer anticipate that it's going to be a lot, you can avert disaster by setting a minimum threshold for the amount of free space. For example, if there's only a couple of K available on the disk, you can send the user a message telling him or her to put a fresh diskette into the floppy drive.

   This function calculates free space on the disk in terms of bytes, which it returns as a long integer (necessary since the under-64K disk deservedly died of obsolescence long ago). While furnishing a useful utility, it also demonstrates the utilization of results returned by the dskparms function in the last section.

*Parameters:*

   drive is an integer (*not* a letter!), in which Ø indicates the default drive, 1 = A, 2 = B, etc.

*Type of Value Returned:*   long (when Ø indicates that either the specified drive does not exist, or else there is, in fact, no space on the disk).

*Other Functions Called:*   dskparms.

```
long diskspc ( drive )          /* free disk space in bytes */
int  drive;
{
    int     tmp [ 4 ];
    long    bpc;

        dskparms ( drive, tmp );
        if ( tmp [ 0 ] == 65535 )
            return ( 0 );           /* invalid drive */
        bpc = ( long ) ( tmp [ 0 ] * tmp [ 2 ] );
        return ( bpc * tmp [ 1 ] );
}
```

# CHAPTER **5**

# Algebraic Functions

$W$e now turn our attention to various functions useful in performing algebraic computations by computer. Some of these routines are commonplace and simply fill in the obvious deficiencies in the C language, such as the absence of powers and roots. Many, however, are fairly exotic, and unless you do a lot of heavyweight scientific programming, you'll probably find that you can go on living without some of them. They're here for math programmers and for those who bump against a rarified calculation now and then. Also, a few functions given later in the book call some of those presented in this chapter.

We need to discuss a few assumptions. The first is that your C product conforms to the Kernighan and Ritchie (K&R) standard with regard to passing floating-point parameters (since the functions in this book adhere to the standard). Some C products furnish floating-point operations, but not according to standard C. In Supersoft C, for example, you can do all the expected things with floating-point numbers, but it takes special, unique calls to Supersoft's own library to do them. As an illustration, to add two floating-point numbers, you can't use the ordinary "+" operator, but instead must call the Supersoft Badd function with address parameters pointing to the target and the addends, all of which must be of type double. If your C compiler does things like this and thus doesn't support floating-point math in a standard fashion, you'll be hard-pressed to find anything here or in any other extensive treatment of the C language that will work for you. (I might add that if you're a serious C programmer, you should invest in a compiler that conforms to the K&R standard or is Unix-compatible, both of which mean the same thing.)

The second assumption is that your compiler came with a library that furnishes essential transcendental functions such as `log`, `exp`, `sqrt`, etc. These are crucial to all algebra in programs. Chances are that any C product conforming to the K&R standard will include them. (*Note*: It's especially important to pay attention to this if you have an IBM PC or compatible with an 8087 coprocessor, as it affects the linker command line with regard to the standard library.)

The third item is as much a recommendation as an assumption, and that is that you use numeric variables of type `double` and not `float` in your calculations. The `float` type in C is a solution in search of a problem; it serves no discernible purpose. One might make a case for memory conservation, inasmuch as a `float` variable takes half the space of a `double`. If you're that tight on memory, however, it's time to buy more. Though `double` uses more memory, it makes programs more efficient since, according to the K&R standard (page 184), "floating arithmetic in C is carried out in double-precision; whenever a `float` appears in an expression it is lengthened to `double` by zero-padding its fraction." In other words, every time it wants to do something to a `float`, the processor has to sidetrack to make it a `double`. This wastes time unnecessarily. Accordingly, all the functions appearing here use only the numeric types `int` and `double`. You won't find a `float` anywhere in this book.

The fourth and final assumption is that you understand what these functions do when described in mathematical terminology. This is a programming book, not a math text, so we won't use valuable space explaining the purpose, theory, and possible applications of specific functions. Chances are that if you don't see what good a particular function is, you don't need it, so you might as well bypass it.

If you do little real "number-crunching" in your programs, I suggest you incorporate into your library the functions called `root` and `ipower` and skip the rest. If you find that you need other functions presented later that call some you omitted, you can always come back here and add them to your library.

These are the algebraic functions in this chapter, grouped by functional area:

## Fundamental group

| | |
|---|---|
| odd | Determines if an integer is an odd number. |
| even | Determines if an integer is an even number. |
| root | *n*th root of a number. |
| ipower | integral power of a value. |
| fpower | Floating-point power of a value. |

## Series

| | |
|---|---|
| fibon | Sum of a Fibonacci series. |
| factrl | Product of a factorial series. |

## Quadratic equations

| | |
|---|---|
| qroots | Root(s) of a quadratic equation. |
| qlow | Low point of a quadratic parabola. |
| q__yplot | *y* coordinate of a given *x*. |
| q__xplot | *x* coordinate(s) of a given *y*. |

## Matrix group

| | |
|---|---|
| m__rswap | Swap two rows of a matrix. |
| m__cswap | Swap two columns of a matrix. |
| minor | Determinant of a 2 × 2 matrix. |
| m__add | Add two matrices. |
| m__sub | Subtract one matrix from another. |
| m__mult | Multiply a matrix by a single value. |
| mxm | Multiply two matrices. |
| det | Determinant of a matrix. |

## Linear equations

| | |
|---|---|
| l__yplot | *y* coordinate given *x*. |
| l__xplot | *x* coordinate given *y*. |
| slope | Slope of a line. |
| x__int | *x*-intercept of a line. |
| y__int | *y*-intercept of a line. |
| l__sfe | Construct standard-form equation from two points. |
| sle2 | Solution to simultaneous linear equations in two unknowns. |
| gauss | Solution to systems of linear equations in multiple unknowns. |

# Fundamental group

### odd

## (quantity)

*Description:*   This function parallels one similarly named in Pascal. It evaluates an integer passed as the quantity parameter to determine whether it's an odd number or not. If not, the function returns logical FALSE (the integer Ø); if the number is odd, it returns logical TRUE (any nonzero integer, 1 in this case).

*Parameters:*   quantity is the integer to be evaluated.

*Type of Value Returned:*   An integer indicating whether quantity is odd (1) or even Ø).

*Other Functions Called:*   None.

*Remarks:*   The "%" is the modulo operator, which furnishes the remainder after division of an integer by an integer.

```
int     odd ( qty )        /* determine if qty is odd */
int     qty;               /* return 0 if even, 1 if odd */
{
    return ( qty % 2 );
}
```

**even**

## (quantity)

*Description:* It will probably come as no shock that this function is the opposite of odd. When quantity is even, it returns 1 (logical TRUE); when it's not even, it returns FALSE (∅).

*Parameters:* quantity is the integer to be evaluated.

*Type of Value Returned:* An integer indicating whether quantity is even (1) or odd (∅).

*Other Functions Called:* None.

```
int    even ( qty )          /* determine if qty is even */
int    qty;                  /* return 1 if even, 0 if not */
{
    int    result;

        return (( qty % 2 ) ? 0 : 1 );
}
```

## root

## ( value, n )

***Description:*** This function computes and returns the *n*th root of value. Both arguments must be doubles. Consequently, it's able to find not only integral but also fractional roots: the 3.184th root of 27.5497, for example. Like human mathematicians, computers are unable to calculate the roots of negative numbers; unlike people, however, computers have no symbolic notation for representing imaginary numbers. As a result, root returns 0 (zero) when value is negative, thereby preventing the program from crashing due to an error. Since 0 cannot be any root of any value except 0, it's easy to check in the program to see whether an error has occurred (you tried to find the root of a negative number), or whether the 0 is, in fact, the result of a legitimate parameter (0.0).

***Parameters:***

value is a double whose root is to be found.
n is a double giving the index (power or exponent) of the root.

***Type of Value Returned:*** double.

***Other Functions Called:*** None.

***Remarks:*** This function, as given here, assumes that any value less than $1.0^{-6}$ (0.000001) is too small to have its root computed.

```
double root ( value, n )          /* nth root of value */
double   value, n;
{
    double    log (), exp ();

        if ( value < 1.0e-6 )
            return ( 0.0 );        /* value too small or negative */
        return ( exp ( log ( value ) / n ));
}
```

# ipower

## ( value, n )

***Description:*** This is the first of two power functions. It returns the integral *n*th power of **value**; that is, **n** must be an integer exponent. The **value** parameter is a **double**. Either or both parameters can be negative numbers and the function will perform as expected under the rules of integral powers. For example, $-9.1$ squared returns $+82.81$ and $-9.1$ cubed results in $-753.571$ (the signs "flip" as the power is odd or even), 9.0 to the 0.5 power gives 3.0, etc. **ipower** corrects the C language's lack of an exponentiation operator.

***Parameters:***

> **value** is a **double** to be raised to a power.
> **n** is an integer exponent.

***Type of Value Returned:*** **double**.

***Other Functions Called:*** None.

```
double ipower ( value, n )      /* value to nth integral power */
                                /* use when exponent is an integer */
double    value;
int       n;
{
    double    result;
    int       i, x;

        x = ( n > 0 ) ? n : -n;
        result = 1.0;
        for ( i = x; i > 0; i-- )
            result *= value;
        if ( n < 0 )
            result = 1.0 / result;
        return ( result );
}
```

## fpower

## ( value, n )

**Description:** Like `ipower`, this function raises `value` to the *n*th power. It has, however, different characteristics and a different purpose. In this case, both parameters are `doubles`, allowing you to raise a number to a fractional power (27.6144 to the power of 3.1416, for example). This is necessary in both scientific applications and in business programs involving the time value of money. The "gotcha" is that `value` cannot be a negative number, since logarithms are involved in the process. The exponent *can* be negative, in which case, as you might expect, the reciprocal of the power is returned. If you furnish a negative `value`, `ipower` returns 0.0 as an error indicator, thus avoiding a crash of the program. As in the case of `root`, it's a simple matter to check the original `value` to find out, when you get a return of 0.0, whether an error occurred or not (the result is only 0.0 when `value` is 0.0).

**Parameters:**

value is the double to be raised.
n is the exponent, also a double.

**Type of Value Returned:** double.

**Other Functions Called:** None.

**Remarks:** Uses `fabs` for the absolute value of a floating-point number.

```
double fpower ( value, n )          /* nth power of value   */
                /* works only when value is positive  */
                /* use when exponent is float or double */
double    value, n;
{
    int        sign;
    double     result, fabs (), exp (), log ();

        sign = ( n < 0.0 ) ? -1 : 1;
        n = fabs ( n );
        result = exp ( log ( value ) * n );
        if ( sign < 0 )
            result = 1.0 / result;
        return ( result );    /* machine infinity when -value */
}
```

# Series group

## fibon

## ( top )

*Description:*   Unlike most of those in the algebra grouping, fibon is strictly an integer function. It returns the sum of the Fibonacci series through top. That is, if top = 4, fibon returns the sum of $1 + 2 + 3 + 4 = 10$. The function returns Ø when top is less than 1, since that is the minimum in Fibonacci numbers.

*Parameters:*   top is an integer giving the highest addend in the Fibonacci series.

*Type of Value Returned:*   The integer sum of the series.

*Other Functions Called:*   None.

```
int fibon ( top )          /* Fibonacci series */
int     top;
{
    int     sum, i;

        if ( top < 1 )
            return ( 0 );
        for ( i = top; i > 0; i-- )
            sum += i;
        return ( sum );
}
```

## factrl

## (top)

*Description:*   The `factrl` function returns the product of a factorial series through `top`, the highest multiplier of the series. To compute 7!, the call is

> prod = factrl (7);

Because factorials tend to increase very rapidly to enormous numbers, the value returned is a **double** even though factorial products are always integers by their nature.

*Parameters:*   `top` is an integer representing the terminal multiplier of the factorial series.

*Type of Value Returned:*   double.

*Other Functions Called:*   None.

*Remarks:*   The returned value is 0.0 when `top` is less than 1, which is the minimum product of a factorial series.

```
double factrl ( top )        /* product of factorial series */
int      top;
{
    double    result;
    int       i;

        if ( top < 1 )
            return ( 0 );
        result = 1;
        for ( i = top; i > 1; i-- )
            result *= i;
        return ( result );
}
```

# Quadratic Equations

The next four functions have to do with solving various aspects of quadratic equations, which have the general form

$$Ax^2 + Bx + C = 0$$

Such equations are always plotted as parabolas with the open end upward, and they can have from zero to two roots (points where they cross the $x$ axis of the graph).

All of the functions given here require that you pass them an array of doubles containing the three coefficients of the quadratic equation. Other parameters are also needed in two of the functions, and they return their results in various ways that are discussed in their descriptions. The coefficients are the basic information needed by any quadratic function to do its job. In this case, the coefficients are arranged in left-to-right order in a three-element array starting at index Ø, such that:

```
coeff[Ø] = A;
coeff[1] = B;
coeff[2] = C;
```

If any term is missing from the equation, as in $3x^2 + 9 = 0$, where the second term is absent, substitute 0 in the array, which in this case becomes the coefficient set (3, 0, 9). When a term has no coefficient— the second term in $5x^2 + x + 2 = 0$, for example—use 1 at its position in the array.

In general, the functions return Ø when there is no solution. As an example, if the plot of a quadratic equation never crosses the $x$ axis, the equation has no roots. Consequently, qroots returns Ø in this case.

Now for the functions themselves.

## qroots

### (coefficients, roots)

*Description:* The qroots function computes and returns (1) the number of roots (Ø to 2) of the quadratic equation and (2) the values of those roots, which are the coordinate(s) of the point(s) where the equation plot crosses an axis. The number of roots is returned directly by the function as an integer; Ø does not mean an error in this case, but simply that the equation has no roots. The values of the roots are returned indirectly in the roots array, where the function writes them into elements Ø and 1. Your program can use the returned integer to find out how many roots to retrieve from this array. If there are no roots, both values will be Ø.Ø; if one, it will be in roots [Ø], and roots [1] will contain Ø.Ø.

*Parameters:*

> coefficients is a three-element array of double containing the coefficients of the quadratic equation as discussed earlier.
> roots is a two-element array of double where the function will write the values of the roots.

*Type of Value Returned:* An integer between Ø and 2 indicating the number of root values written into the roots array.

*Other Functions Called:* None.

```
int     qroots ( cf, roots )     /* finds roots of quadratic equation */
double  cf [], roots [];         /* returns number of roots as int    */
                                 /* results returned in 'roots' array */
{
    double    dis, sqrt ();

        roots [ 0 ] = roots [ 1 ] = 0;
        if ( cf [ 0 ] == 0.0 )        /* no solution */
            return ( 0 );
        dis = ( cf [ 1 ] * cf [ 1 ] ) - ( 4 * cf [ 0 ] * cf [ 2 ] );
        if ( dis < 0.0 )
            return ( 0 );             /* no roots */
        dis = sqrt ( dis );
        roots [ 0 ] = ( -cf [ 1 ] + dis ) / ( 2. * cf [ 0 ] );
        if ( dis == 0.0 )
            return ( 1 );
        roots [ 1 ] = ( -cf [ 1 ] - dis ) / ( 2. * cf [ 0 ] );
        return ( 2 );
}
```

## (coefficients, coordinates)

***Description:*** Because the plot of a quadratic equation always produces a parabola pointing downward, there is for every equation a "low point" representing the absolute bottom of the curve, or in other words, the smallest possible value of *y*. The low point expresses this location as *x* and *y* coordinates; any *x* smaller or greater than that of the low point will resolve to a *y* that is greater. The qlow function calculates this point and returns it indirectly in the coordinates array. It does not return any value directly.

***Parameters:***

> coefficients is an array of double containing the coefficients of the equation as discussed earlier.
> roots is an array of double where the function stores its results. Upon return, roots [Ø] contains the low point's *x* coordinate and roots [1] its *y*.

***Type of Value Returned:*** None directly.

***Other Functions Called:*** None.

***Remarks:*** This function can cause a program crash due to division by zero if the coefficient of the first ($x^2$) term is Ø.Ø. In that case, the equation is not a quadratic, so this potential problem should never occur.

```
qlow ( cf, coords )        /* low point of quadratic graph */
double   cf [], coords [];   /* return coords in array */
{
    double    x;

        x  = -cf [ 1 ] / ( 2.0 * cf [ 0 ] );
        coords [ 0 ] = x;
        coords [ 1 ] = ( cf [ 0 ] * x * x ) + ( cf [ 1 ] * x ) + cf [ 2 ];
}
```

## **q__yplot**

## (x, coefficients)

***Description:*** For any given value of *x* in a quadratic equation, there is a corresponding *y*. This function takes the *x* and the coefficients and returns the *y* where the plot crosses that *x*. In effect it solves the quadratic equation for a specific *x* coordinate. Use q__yplot both for obtaining values from the equation and also for graphics programs that plot quadratic curves. In the latter case, it will usually be necessary to convert the *x* and the double result into an integer.

***Parameters:***

    x is a double giving the *x* coordinate.
    coefficients is a three-element array of double containing the coefficients as discussed above.

***Type of Value Returned:*** double giving the *y* corresponding to the *x* passed as a parameter.

***Other Functions Called:*** None.

***Remarks:*** The parabolic nature of quadratic curves increases *y* at a much greater rate than *x* increases. Consequently, although there is in theory a *y* for every possible *x*, large values of *x* may force *y* beyond the ability of the double type to represent it, in which case the program will probably crash on an overflow error. The function cannot, as a practical matter, predict and avoid such situations, so the best I can do is warn you.

```
double q_yplot ( x, cf )        /* compute y of quadratic equation,   */
double    x, cf [];             /* given value of x and coefficients */
{
    double    y;

        y = (( cf [ 0 ] * x * x ) + ( cf [ 1 ] * x ) + cf [ 2 ] );
        return ( y );
}
```

## q__xplot

## (y, coefficients, coordinates)

*Description:*   In a sense, this function is the opposite of q__yplot presented above in that it solves the quadratic equation "backward" by furnishing the value(s) of *x*, if any, that satisfy a given y. Because a quadratic equation produces a parabola closed at the bottom, for any vertical location (*y*) above the low point there are two *x*'s representing the left and right sides of the parabola. At the low point, there is only one *x*, that being the end of the parabola, and below the low point there is no solution since the curve doesn't exist. q__xplot, then, returns an integer indicating the number of *x* coordinates for the given *y*, and places them in the coordinates array where the calling program can fetch them. The *x*'s are not in any particular order (left-to-right or vice versa). Like q__yplot, this function is useful both for mathematical purposes and for graphics plotting.

*Parameters:*

> y is a double giving the y to solve for.
> coefficients is a three-element array of double giving the coefficients as discussed earlier.
> coordinates is an array of double consisting of a minimum of two elements, where the function is to store its results (the *x* coordinates).

*Type of Value Returned:*   An integer indicating how many *x* coordinates the function has placed in the coordinates array.

*Other Functions Called:*   qroots.

*Remarks:*   This function "tricks" qroots by modifying the coefficients and thus displacing the x axis upward or downward to the position of y. Before returning to the calling program, it restores the coefficients array to its initial set of values, so that the coefficient values are unchanged upon return.

```
int q_xplot ( y, cf, cy )      /* compute x's for given y */
double y, cf [], cy [];        /* in a quadratic equation */
{
    int     n;

        cf [ 2 ] -= y;
        n = ( qroots ( cf, cy ));
        cf [ 2 ] += y;              /* restore coefficients */
        return ( n );
}
```

# Matrix group

## m__rswap

### ( matrix, ra, rb, ncols )

*Description:* This function and the following perform elementary transformations on matrices by exchanging their rows (m__rswap) and their columns (see m__cswap). Unlike the other matrix functions in this section, they actually modify the matrix passed as a parameter. Generally, matrices retain the same value for purposes of operations performed on them if two or more rows are swapped, and in some applications they are also equivalent when columns are switched. Swapping rows or columns is a convenience for rearranging matrices in applications (such as Gauss elimination, which solves systems of simultaneous linear equations in multiple unknowns), and commonly occurs in other matrix manipulations.

*Parameters:*

matrix is the name of any matrix of double in which two rows are to be swapped.

ra and rb are the integral numbers of the rows being swapped, where the first row is Ø.

ncols is the integral number of columns across the width of the matrix.

*Type of Value Returned:* None (modifies matrix directly).

*Other Functions Called:* None.

*Remarks:* This function cannot verify that the row numbers are valid for the given matrix, nor that it has the number of columns specified in ncols. Failure to pass correct values in these parameters will produce garbage and wreak havoc with your matrix.

```
m_rswap ( mat, ra, rb, ncols )     /* swap two rows in matrix */
double    mat [];
int       ra, rb, ncols;
{
    int    .  c, x1, x2;
    double  t;

        if ( ncols > 0 )
            for ( c = 0; c < ncols; c++ ) {
                x1 = ( ra * ncols ) + c;
                x2 = ( rb * ncols ) + c;
                t = mat [ x1 ];
                mat [ x1 ] = mat [ x2 ];
                mat [ x2 ] = t;
            }
}
```

## m___cswap

## ( matrix, ca, cb, nrows )

***Description:*** This function is very similar to **m___rswap** in the preceding section, except that it swaps two columns in the named matrix. The same discussion applies to both functions.

***Parameters:***

> **matrix** is the name of a matrix of **double** in which two columns are to be exchanged.
> **ca** and **cb** are integers giving the column numbers to be swapped, where Ø is the leftmost column.
> **nrows** is the number of rows in the matrix.

***Type of Value Returned:*** None (modifies **matrix** directly).

***Other Functions Called:*** None.

***Remarks:*** See Remarks for **m___rswap**.

```
m_cswap ( mat, ca, cb, nrows )    /* swap two cols in matrix */
double    mat [];
int       ca, cb, nrows;
{
    int       r, x1, x2;
    double    t;

        if ( nrows > 0 )
            for ( r = 0; r < nrows; r++ ) {
                x1 = ( r * nrows ) + ca;
                x2 = ( r * nrows ) + cb;
                t = mat [ x1 ];
                mat [ x1 ] = mat [ x2 ];
                mat [ x2 ] = t;
            }
}
```

## minor

## ( matrix )

***Description:*** This function returns the determinant of a 2 × 2 matrix, which it obtains by cross multiplying the elements and subtracting the second product from the first. A minor is not itself of any great importance in mathematics, but it is the bedrock of more complex matrix operations. Consequently, minor is called by other functions that appear later in this chapter, and it is important to those operations.

***Parameters:*** matrix is the name of a 2 × 2 array of double.

***Type of Value Returned:*** A double representing the minor of the matrix.

***Other Functions Called:*** None.

```
double minor ( matrix )      /* determinant of 2 x 2 matrix */
double  matrix [ ];
{
    double    result;

        result  = matrix [ 0 ] * matrix [ 3 ];
        result -= matrix [ 2 ] * matrix [ 1 ];
        return ( result );
}
```

## m_add

## ( a, b, c, rows, cols )

**Description:** This function adds two matrices together and places their sum in matrix $C$ ($A + B = C$). Consistent with the rules of matrix addition, both involved matrices must be of the same dimensions, and the result also has those dimensions. The matrices used with m_add are all doubles. The function returns an integer that is Ø if it could not perform; otherwise, it returns the total number of elements in any given array.

A couple of things need to be noted here. They apply also to the m_sub (matrix subtraction) function that follows. First, the matrices you pass as parameters will usually be two-dimensional, but you can also add one-dimensional arrays. The function will operate properly if you set either the rows or columns parameter to 1 and use the other of these parameters to show the number of elements per array.

Although the matrices as passed are usually two-dimensional, the addition and subtraction functions regard them as having only one dimension. The functions themselves use the rows and columns parameters to affect two-dimensional indexing and to "keep their place" within the matrices. Although this adds some overhead, it is the only way to deal effectively in C with matrices having dimensions that vary from one call to the next.

The indexing "trick" permits you to add matrices of any dimensions—$1 \times 2$ or $500 \times 800$ or whatever—so long as both additive matrices have the same dimensions.

**Parameters:**

a is a matrix of double to be added to b.

b is a matrix of double to be added to a.

c is a matrix of double where the m_add will place the sum of matrices a and b.

rows is an integer giving the number of rows in the matrices.

cols is an integer giving the number of columns in the matrices.

**Type of Value Returned:** Integer (Ø when rows or cols specified a zero value, meaning the matrices are empty and could not be added; otherwise, the total number of elements per matrix).

**Other Functions Called:** None.

***Remarks:*** The function has no way of determining whether the parameters specify *more* rows or columns than a given matrix has. It is your responsibility to make sure the parameters are within the dimensions of the matrices; failure to do so will yield mighty strange results.

```
int m_add ( a, b, c, rows, cols )      /* add two matrices */
double  a [], b [], c [];
int     rows, cols;
{
    int         e, x;
    register    r, i;

        if ( rows <= 0 || cols <= 0 )
            return ( 0 );                /* can't do it */
        e = 0;
        for ( r = 0; r < rows; r++ ) {
            for ( i = 0; i < cols, i++ ) {
                x = ( r * cols ) + i;    /* index to array */
                c [ x ] = a [ x ] + b [ x ];
                e++;
            }
        }
        return ( e );
}
```

## m_sub

## ( a, b, c, rows, cols )

***Description:*** This function is very similar to m_add in the preceding section, and virtually everything discussed there applies here. The difference is that m_sub, as its name suggests, performs matrix subtraction ($A - B =\, C$) on two identically sized matrices.

***Parameters:***

> a is a matrix of double.
> b is a matrix of double to be subtracted from a.
> c is a matrix of double where the m_sub will place the difference of $A - B$.
> rows is an integer giving the number of rows in the matrices.
> cols is an integer giving the number of columns in the matrices.

***Type of Value Returned:*** Integer (Ø if rows or columns specified a zero value, meaning the matrices are empty and could not be subtracted; otherwise, the number of elements per matrix).

***Other Functions Called:*** None.

***Remarks:*** See remarks for m_add.

```
int m_sub ( a, b, c, rows, cols )   /* subtract mat b from a */
double   a [], b [], c [];
int      rows, cols;
{
    int      r, i, e, x;

        if ( rows <= 0 || cols <= 0 )
            return ( 0 );                        /* can't do it */
        e = 0;
        for ( r = 0; r < rows; r++ ) {
            for ( i = 0; i < cols; i++ ) {
                x = ( r * cols ) + i;    /* index to array */
                c [ x ] = a [ x ] - b [ x ];
                e++;
            }
        }
        return ( e );
}
```

## m_mult

### ( value, matrix, result, rows, cols )

*Description:* This function multiplies an entire matrix of double by a single double value, as in the equation

$$ \text{value} \times \mid \text{matrix} \mid \; = \; \mid \text{result} \mid $$

That is, for example, if value is 2.5, each element of matrix is multiplied by 2.5, and the products are put into the appropriate locations in result, which is an array of the same dimensions as matrix. Be careful not to confuse this function with mxm in the following section, which multiplies two matrices.

*Parameters:*

value is a double giving the single value by which matrix is to be multiplied.

matrix is the matrix containing the original array of double numbers to be multiplied by value.

result is a matrix of the same dimensions as matrix, in which the products of multiplication are to be returned by the function (it can be the same array as matrix, but of course this alters the original values).

rows is an integer specifying the number of rows in both matrix and result.

cols is an integer specifying the number of columns in both matrix and result.

*Type of Value Returned:* None.

*Other Functions Called:* None.

*Remarks:* This function, like the other matrix functions, does not and cannot verify that the specified number of rows and columns is valid. If invalid values are passed as parameters, the result will probably be garbage, and the function may corrupt adjacent data storage areas as well.

```
    /* multiply mat by single value giving result */
m_mult ( value, mat, result, rows, cols )
double   value, mat [], result [];
int      rows, cols;
{
    int    x, r, c;

        for ( r = 0; r < rows; r++ ) {
            for ( c = 0; c < cols; c++ ) {
                x = ( r * cols ) + c;
                result [ x ] = mat [ x ] * value;
            }
        }
}
```

**mxm**

# ( a, b, c, arows, acols, bcols )

***Description:*** This function multiplies one matrix (*a*) by another matrix (*b*) and places the resulting matrix in *c*. In order to multiply one matrix by another, the second matrix (*b*) has to have the same number of *rows* as the first (*a*) has of *columns*. This common dimension is given by the `Acols` parameter. The number of rows in *a* and the number of columns in *b* can be any values greater than Ø. The size of the resulting matrix (*c*) is `arows` by `bcols`, for example:

$$\begin{vmatrix} 1 & 2 & -3 \\ 4 & 0 & -2 \end{vmatrix} \quad \begin{vmatrix} 5 & -4 & 2 & 0 \\ -1 & 6 & 3 & 1 \\ 7 & 0 & 4 & 8 \end{vmatrix} = \begin{vmatrix} -18 & 8 & -4 & -22 \\ 6 & -16 & 0 & -16 \end{vmatrix}$$

$$\text{A} \qquad \times \qquad \text{B} \qquad = \qquad \text{C}$$

In this case, *a* has two rows by three columns and *b* has three rows by four columns (rows in *a* = columns in *b*). As a result, their product *c* has dimensions of two rows by four columns.

The declarations for the matrices in the example are:

`double        a [2] [3]`, `b [3] [4]`, `c [2] [4];`

***Parameters:***

a is a matrix of `double` to be multiplied.

b is a matrix of `double` that is the multiplier. It must have the same number of columns as a has of rows.

c is a matrix of `double` where the result will be placed. It must have the same number of rows as a and the same number of columns as b.

arows is the integral number of rows in a.

acols is the integral number of columns in a and also the number of rows in b.

bcols is the integral number of columns in b.

***Type of Value Returned:*** None (results returned in c).

***Other Functions Called:*** None.

***Remarks:*** mxm has no way of determining whether the receiving matrix c is properly sized to accommodate the results. This is your responsibility.

```
  mxm ( a, b, c, ar, ac, bc )        /* multiply two matrices */
double  a [], b [], c [];
int     ar, ac, bc;
{
    int         x1, x2, x3, v4, v5;
    register    v1, v2, v3;

        for ( v1 = 0; v1 < ar; v1++ ) {
            for ( v2 = 0; v2 < bc; v2++ ) {
                x1 = ( v1 * bc ) + v2;
                    c [ x1 ]  0.0;
                    for ( v3 = 0; v3 < ac; v3++ ) {
                        x2 = ( v1 * ac ) + v3;
                        x3 = ( v3 * bc ) + v2;
                        c [ x1 ] += a [ x2 ] * b [ x3 ];
                    }
            }
        }
}
```

# det

## ( mat, order )

*Description:* The det function returns the determinant of a square matrix of any order greater than Ø. If the order is 1 (that is, the matrix is one row by one column, or in other words, a single value), det returns that value; for any larger matrix, it uses the expansion theorem for determinants, expanding by cofactors of the first row.

In one of my previous books, *Practical Programming in Pascal* (New York: Plume, 1984), I stated that I consider recursion faddish, overrated and seldom of much use. I stick by that position, but every once in a while you do find a process that is inherently recursive, and solving a matrix greater than order 3 for its determinant is one of them. As a result, det utilizes recursion to resolve a plethora of minors of diminishing size. In general, the number of recursive calls equals the square of the order, so if the matrix is 4 × 4, it takes 16 calls to calculate the determinant; if 5 × 5, 25 calls, etc. Also, because the function uses dynamic storage allocation to pass minors from one level to another, the amount of memory consumed by the function increases geometrically with the order of the matrix. This raises the possibility, in large matrices, of running out of memory. When that happens, det halts program with the message "ERROR: Out of memory in det ()."

*Parameters:*

mat is the name of a square matrix of double.
order is an integer giving the number of rows (or columns) in
matrix.

*Type of Value Returned:* A double representing the determinant of the square matrix contained in mat.

*Other Functions Called:* even, minor, det.

*Remarks:* The function assumes but cannot verify that mat is a square matrix; if it is not, you will get bizarre results. Though its listing is not long considering the amount of work it does, recursion may cause the function to run for a substantial time before it returns a result, and consume large amounts of memory in the process. It does free all memory it allocated.

```
double det ( mat, order )     /* determinant of matrix */
double mat [];
int     order;
{
    int       p, even (), r, c, n, x;
    double    *mark, *cof, *calloc (),
              d, val, minor (), det ();

        d = 0.0;
        if ( order == 1 )
            return ( mat [ 0 ] );
        if ( order == 2 )
            return ( minor ( mat ));
        for ( p = 0; p < order; p++ ) {
            n = ( order - 1 ) * ( order - 1 );
            mark = cof = ( double *) (calloc ( n, sizeof ( double )));
            if ( cof == 0 ) {
                puts ( "\nERROR: out of memory in det ()" );
                exit ( 1 );
            }
            for ( r = 1; r < order; r++ ) {    /* copy minor */
                for ( c = 0; c < order; c++ ) {
                    if ( c != p ) {
                        x = ( r * order ) + c;
                        *cof++ = mat [ x ];
                    }
                }
            }
            val = det ( mark, order - 1 );    /* recursive call */
            d += (( even ( p )) ? val : -val ) * mat [ p ];
            free ( cof );
        }
        return ( d );
}
```

# Linear Equations

Linear equations have the general form

$$Ax + By + C = 0$$

They are called linear equations because their plots always form a straight line when drawn on a graph. Many scientific and business problems have to do with the solutions to linear equations, and consequently they form an important part of the algebraic library for serious programmers. This section deals with linear equations in two unknowns ($x$ and $y$). The last section of the chapter covers systems of linear equations in multiple unknowns.

The approach to the linear functions is pretty much the same as to the quadratics; you must pass an array of double containing the three coefficients in the order:

```
coeff[0] = A;
coeff[1] = B;
coeff[2] = C;
```

Substitute 1 when there is no coefficient (coeff[0] = 1 when $x + 3y + 2 = 0$). An equation is not linear if either the $x$ or $y$ term is missing, but a linear equation can omit the $C$, as in $5x - 3y = 0$. In that case, coeff[2] = 0.

## ( x, coefficients )

***Description:*** The l_yplot function returns the *y* coordinate for any *x* in a linear equation. It merely "plugs" the *x* into the equation using its coefficients and calculates the corresponding *y*, which it returns as a double. The function returns 0.0 under two circumstances:

1. The *y* coordinate for the given *x* is in fact 0.0.
2. The equation is not linear (lacks a *y* term). This is an error condition.

***Parameters:***

x is the *x* coordinate for which the corresponding *y* is to be found.
coefficients is a three-element array of double containing the coefficients of the linear equation being solved.

***Type of Value Returned:*** double.

***Other Functions Called:*** None.

```
double l_yplot ( x, cf )    /* plot y of linear equation */
double x, cf [];
{
    if ( cf [ 1 ] == 0.0 )
        return ( 0.0 );         /* no solution */
    return ((( -cf [ 0 ] * x ) - cf [ 2 ] ) / cf [ 1 ] );
}
```

## l_xplot

## ( y, coefficients )

**Description:**   This function has exactly the opposite effect of l_yplot presented previously. That is, given a $y$ coordinate and the coefficients of the linear equation, it returns the corresponding $x$. Everything else about it is the same.

**Parameters:**

y is the $y$ coordinate for which the corresponding $x$ is to be found.
coefficients is a three-element array of double containing the coefficients of the linear equation being solved.

**Type of Value Returned:**   double.

**Other Functions Called:**   None.

```
double l_xplot ( x, cf )    /* plot x of linear equation */
double x, cf [];
{
    if ( cf [ 0 ] == 0.0 )
        return ( 0.0 );          /* no solution */
    return ((( -cf [ 1 ] * x ) - cf [ 2 ] ) / cf [ 0 ] );
}
```

## slope

## (x1, y1, x2, y2 )

**Description:**   Slope is a common function throughout mathematics. In essence, it is the ratio of vertical change to horizontal: "How many units does the line move up or down for every unit of horizontal motion?" It is particularly useful in working with linear equations, hence its inclusion here. The slope function returns a double value derived from the $x$ and $y$ coordinates (also doubles) of two points along a line described by a linear equation, according to standard methods.

**Parameters:**

x1 and y1 are the coordinates of one point.
x2 and y2 are the coordinates of the other point.
Both sets of coordinates are doubles.

**Type of Value Returned:**   double.

**Other Functions Called:**   None.

**Remarks:**   A horizontal line has no slope and thus returns a 0.0 value. This is not an error. A vertical line has an infinite slope (the result of division by zero). Since this is intolerable to a computer, the function returns the value 9.9e+32 when the slope is predicted to be infinite. This is an extremely large value that will usually serve satisfactorily and introduce only negligible errors into subsequent calculations. If your compiler supports a larger "machine infinity" value, use it.

```
double  slope ( x1, y1, x2, y2 )     /* slope of a line */
double  x1, y1, x2, y2;
{
    if (( x2 - x1 ) == 0.0 )
        return ( 9.9e+32 );          /* vertical */
    return (( y2 - y1 ) / ( x2 - x1 ));
}
```

## x_int

## ( coefficients )

*Description:*   This function, useful both in solutions to linear equations and in geometry, finds the *x* intercept of a line; that is, the *x* coordinate where the line described by a linear equation passes through the *x* axis. It uses the coefficients of the standard-form linear equation to develop the answer, which is returned directly by the function as a double.

*Parameters:*   coefficients is a three-element array of double containing the coefficients of the linear equation.

*Type of Value Returned:*   double.

*Other Functions Called:*   None.

*Remarks:*   If the line is horizontal, it never intercepts the *x* axis, and consequently this function returns the "infinite" value 9.9e + 32. See Remarks for slope for more discussion. (*Note:* If your compiler has a greater "infinity," use it instead.)

```
double x_int ( cf )       /* x intercept of linear equation */
double cf [];
{
    if ( cf [ 0 ] == 0.0 )
        return ( 9.9e+32 );       /* horizontal (no x_int) */
    return ( -cf [ 2 ] / cf [ 0 ] );
}
```

## y__int

## ( coefficients )

*Description:* Similar in all other respects to x__int in the preceding section, this function returns the $y$ intercept of a line defined by a linear equation, that is, where the line crosses the $y$ axis.

*Parameters:* coefficients is a three-element array of double containing the coefficients of the linear equation.

*Type of Value Returned:* double.

*Other Functions Called:* None.

*Remarks:* If the line is vertical, it never intercepts the $y$ axis, and consequently this function returns the "infinite" value $9.9e+32$. See Remarks for slope for more discussion.

```
double y_int ( cf )      /* y intercept of linear equation */
double cf [];
{
    if ( cf [ 1 ] == 0.0 )
        return ( 9.9e+32 );       /* vertical (no y_int) */
    return ( -cf [ 2 ] / cf [ 1 ] );
}
```

## ( x1, y1, x2, y2, coefficients )

***Description:*** Given the coordinates of two points, l_sfe constructs the linear standard-form equation (the function name is an acronym) that satisfies those points. It returns the results in the coefficients array whose name or starting address is passed to it as a parameter. This array must be of double and contain at least three elements. The function loads the array with coefficients in the expected order (*A*, *B*, and *C*). Note that it makes no attempt to find integral coefficients, which means it doesn't return "textbook" solutions. For example, given the coordinates $(-2, 1)$ and $(2, 3)$, the returned coefficients are $-0.5$, 1 and $-2$, which if plugged into the standard form of the equation give

$$-0.5 \, x + y - 2 = 0$$

This is exactly equivalent to, but not as elegant as,

$$- \, x + 2y - 4 = 0$$

which is the form favored in mathematics texts.

***Parameters:***

x1, y1 are type double coordinates of one point on the line.
x2, y2 are another coordinate pair on the same line.
coefficients is the name of a three-element array of double where the function places the resulting coefficients.

***Type of Value Returned:*** None directly.

***Other Functions Called:*** slope.

```
l_sfe ( x1, y1, x2, y2, cf )        /* find coeffs of linear */
double       x1, y1, x2, y2, cf [];   /* eqn given 2 points */
{
    double   sl, slope ();
    int      i;

        for ( i = 0; i < 3; i++ )
            cf [ i ] = 0.0;                 /* initialize */
        if (( sl = slope ( x1, y1, x2, y2 )) == 0 )
            cf [ 1 ] = y1;              /* horizontal */
        else
        if ( sl >= 9.9e+32 )
            cf [ 0 ] = x1;             /*  vertical  */
        else {                          /*  sloping   */
            cf [ 2 ] = -( y1 - ( sl * x1 ));
            cf [ 0 ] = -sl;
            cf [ 1 ] = 1.0;
        }
}
```

## ( coeff1, coeff2, solution )

***Description:*** This function solves a system of simultaneous linear equations in two unknowns, hence its name. It requires the coefficients of two equations, which must be doubles arranged in the usual order in the first two parameter arrays. If the equations have a solution (that is, the lines they define cross), sle2 returns the integer 1 (logical TRUE) and places the coordinates of the solution in the third array, with the $x$ in the element $0$ and the $y$ in element 1. When there is no solution (the lines never cross), the function returns $0$ and the solution array contains zeros.

***Parameters:***

coeff1 is a three-element array of double containing the coefficients of one of the equations.

coeff2 is similar to the one preceding, containing the coefficients of the other equation.

solution is a two-element array of double where the function places the coordinates of the solution as described above.

***Type of Value Returned:*** Integer ($0$ for no solution; 1 if there is a solution).

***Other Functions Called:*** None.

```
int sle2 ( c1, c2, sol )        /* solve 2 linear eqns */
double c1 [], c2 [], sol [];
{
    double    d;

        sol [ 0 ] = sol [ 1 ] = 0.0;
        d = ( c1 [ 1 ] * c2 [ 0 ] ) - ( c1 [ 0 ] * c2 [ 1 ] );
        if ( d == 0.0 )
            return ( 0 );          /* no solution */
        sol [ 0 ] = -(( c1 [ 1 ] * c2 [ 2 ] ) -
                      ( c1 [ 2 ] * c2 [ 1 ] )) / d;
        sol [ 1 ] = -(( c1 [ 2 ] * c2 [ 0 ] ) -
                      ( c1 [ 0 ] * c2 [ 2 ] )) / d;
        return ( 1 );
}
```

## ( coeff, results, n )

*Description:*   The gauss function is so named because it uses the Gauss elimination method for solving systems of simultaneous linear equations in multiple unknowns. This is as much a matrix problem as it is one of linear algebra, in that the function expects a rectangular matrix of $n$ rows by $n + 1$ columns, where $n$ is the number of unknowns in the system of equations. Suppose, for example, that we have the following system of equations:

$$
\begin{aligned}
x \quad\quad - 2z + 2w &= 1 \\
-2x + 3y + 4z \quad\quad &= -1 \\
y + \ z - \ w &= 0 \\
3x + \ y - 2z - \ w &= 3
\end{aligned}
$$

This system has four unknowns ($x$, $y$, $z$, and $w$), thus four equations. The gauss function operates on a matrix of the coefficients and results of these equations, or in this case a $4 \times 5$ matrix. Note that the outcome of each individual equation, such as the 1 to the right of the equals sign in the first equation, must be in the $n + 1$th (rightmost) column. Keeping the coefficients in proper position, mindful of signs, and substituting 0s for missing terms, we get the following matrix:

$$
\begin{array}{rrrrr}
1 & 0 & -2 & 2 & 1 \\
-2 & 3 & 4 & 0 & -1 \\
0 & 1 & 1 & -1 & 0 \\
3 & 1 & -2 & -1 & 3
\end{array}
$$

This matrix becomes the coeff parameter passed to gauss, and the number of unknowns (or rows in the matrix, if you prefer to think of it that way) is 4, passed as the n parameter.

   The function solves for the unknowns and passes them back in results, which must be a one-dimensional array with n elements: four, in this example. The solutions are in the left-to-right order of unknowns from the original system of equations. In this case, after gauss returns control to the calling program, the results array has the following contents:

$$\text{results}[0] = \quad 3 \quad (x)$$
$$\text{results}[1] = -1 \quad (y)$$
$$\text{results}[2] = \quad 2 \quad (z)$$
$$\text{results}[3] = \quad 1 \quad (w)$$

and the original coeff matrix is unchanged.

The function rearranges the equations in an effort to put a nonzero coefficient in each position along the main diagonal, so that the system can be solved. If it is unable to accomplish this after reshuffling $n$ times, or if there is insufficient free memory to accommodate a copy of the original matrix, gauss returns a Ø value directly to signify that it could not solve the equations. Otherwise it returns an integer equal to the number of original unknowns, meaning that it was successful. You can test for this condition with a construct such as

```
if ( gauss ( coeff, results, 4) = 0) {
    ( unsuccessful completion )
} else {
    ( solution is in results array )
}
```

**Parameters:**

coeff is a matrix of double arranged as discussed.

results is a one-dimensional array of double having at least $n$ elements, where gauss puts the solutions to the unknowns.

n is the number of unknowns to solve for. It also specifies the number of rows in the coeff matrix, and the number of columns less one.

***Type of Value Returned:*** Integer. Value is Ø when the function did not complete successfully; otherwise, a nonzero value equal to the number of original unknowns.

***Other Functions Called:*** m__rswap.

***Remarks:*** This function cannot verify that the number of rows in coeff is equal to $n$ and the number of columns is $n + 1$. This is your responsibility. Systems of simultaneous linear equations having fewer or more equations than the number of unknowns cannot properly be solved, and if faced with such a situation, the gauss function is likely to return garbage as results.

```
int gauss ( cf, rm, n )      /* Gauss solution for simultaneous  */
double   cf [], rm [];       /* linear eqns in multiple unknowns */
int      n;
{
    double   *calloc (), *copy, *repl, t;
    int      r, c, x1, x2, nr, nc, z;

        nr = n;                                          /* rows in matrix */
        nc = n + 1;                                      /* cols in matrix */
        if (( repl = copy = calloc (( nr * nc ), sizeof ( double ))) == 0 )
            return ( 0 );
        for ( r = 0; r < nr; r++ )                    /* make copy of mat */
            for ( c = 0; c < nc; c++ ) {
                x1 = ( r * nc ) + c;
                *copy++ = cf [ x1 ];
            }
        x2 = 0;
        z = (( nr - 1 ) * nc ) + nc - 2;
        do {                                /* rearrange rows for eschelon */
            for ( r = 0; r < nr; r++ ) {
                x1 = ( r * nc ) + r;
                for ( c = r; c < nr; c++ ) {
                    if ( cf [ x1 ] == 0.0 && r != c )
                        m_rswap ( cf, r, c, nc );
                }
            }
            if ( cf [ z ] == 0.0 )
                m_rswap ( cf, z, x2, nc );
        } while ( x2++ < nr - 1 );
        for ( r = 0; r < nr; r++ ) {
            x1 = ( r * nc ) + r;
            if ( cf [ x1 ] == 0.0 )
                return ( 0 );                            /* no solution */
        }
                        /* elimination phase */
        for ( r = 0; r < n - 1; r++ )
            for ( z = r + 1; z < n; z++ ) {
                x1 = ( z * nc ) + r;
                x2 = ( r * nc ) + r;
                t  = cf [ x1 ] / cf [ x2 ];              /* elim factor */
                for ( c = 0; c < nc; c++ ) {
                    x1 = ( z * nc ) + c;
                    x2 = ( r * nc ) + c;
                    cf [ x1 ] -= cf [ x2 ] * t;
                }
            }
                    /* backward substitution phase */
        x1 = (( nr - 1 ) * nc ) + n - 1;
        rm [ n - 1 ] = cf [ x1 + 1 ] / cf [ x1 ];    /* last unknown */
        for ( r = n - 2; r >= 0; r-- ) {
            x1 = ( r * nc ) + r;                        /* coeff of unknown */
            t  = cf [ ( r * nc ) + n ];
```

```
            for ( c = r + 1; c < n; c++ ) {
                x2 = ( r * nc ) + c;
                t -= cf [ x2 ] * rm [ c ];
            }
            rm [ r ] = t / cf [ x1 ];            /* solution to factor */    .
        }
        copy = repl;
        for ( r = 0; r < nr; r++ )                /* restore orig matrix */
            for ( c = 0; c < nc; c++ ) {
                x1 = ( r * nc ) + c;
                cf [ x1 ] = *copy++;
            }
        free ( repl );
        return ( n );
    }
```

# CHAPTER 6

# GEOMETRIC AND TRIGONOMETRIC FUNCTIONS

*L*ike the chapter on algebraic functions (Chapter 5), this chapter groups geometric functions by broad categories of application. Except for some of the more arcane trigonometric functions, probably most people have an intuitive understanding of what the majority of these subprograms do but, having been away from the classroom for a while, they've forgotten exactly how they do it. The thrust here, then, is to furnish proven routines that will save you the trouble of dusting off the old textbooks and figuring out how to translate theorems into program code.

These functions, like those in the previous chapter, deal with numeric variables of type `double`. Accordingly, where values are treated as integers in your program—grid coordinates, for example—it's necessary to convert them to `doubles` before passing them as parameters, since type conversion (or promotion, as K&R refers to it) does not automatically occur in external function calls. Also, the functions that return values directly need to be declared as `doubles` in the heading of the calling program in order for the returned values to be in proper format.

Some functions associated with geometry have already been presented in the algebraic chapter: slope, *x* and *y* intercept, solutions to linear and parabolic problems, and so on. There is often a fine line between facets of mathematics, and so some crossover between these two chapters is inevitable.

The following are the contents of this chapter by category, function name, and purpose:

### Basic group:

| | |
|---|---|
| deg2rad | Degrees to radians. |
| rad2deg | Radians to degrees. |

### Coordinate group:

| | |
|---|---|
| distance | Distance between two points. |
| mid_pt | Midpoint coordinates of a line. |

### Circle group:

| | |
|---|---|
| circum | Circumference of a circle. |
| cir_area | Area of a circle. |
| cir_ctr | Define the center of a circle from three points. |
| sph_area | Area of a sphere. |
| sph_vol | Volume of a sphere. |

### Triangle group:

| | |
|---|---|
| rt_area | Area of a right triangle. |
| rt_hyp | Hypoteneuse of a right triangle. |
| rt_side | Side of a right triangle. |
| t_2sia | Solve triangle given two sides, included angle. |
| t_2ais | Solve triangle given two angles, included side. |
| t_3s | Solve triangle given three sides. |

### Trigonometric group

| | |
|---|---|
| tan | Tangent. |
| cot | Cotangent. |
| csc | Cosecant. |
| sec | Secant. |
| sinh | Hyperbolic sine. |
| cosh | Hyperbolic cosine. |
| tanh | Hyperbolic tangent. |
| sech | Hyperbolic secant. |
| csch | Hyperbolic cosecant. |
| coth | Hyperbolic cotangent. |
| arcsin | Inverse sine. |
| arccos | Inverse cosine. |

# Basic group

## deg2rad

### ( degrees )

*Description:*   Hardly anyone except a computer programmer uses radians in calculating angles, and why compiler makers persist in using this obscure measurement is anyone's guess. Yet, almost without exception, every compiler's built-in sine, cosine, and so forth require radians, not degrees. Thus, if you and your software's users are to work in familiar terms, you need a pair of conversion routines to toggle between the "external" world of degrees and the internal insistence on radians. That's what this and the next function do. Specifically, deg2rad converts degrees to radians so that angles can be worked on by your program.

*Parameters:*   degrees is an angle of type double.

*Type of Value Returned:*   double, the equivalent of degrees expressed in radians.

*Other Functions Called:*   None.

*Remarks:*   The angle can be any value, positive or negative. If the absolute value exceeds 360 degrees, the function brings it within the range of plus or minus 360 before converting.

```
double deg2rad ( degrees )        /* degrees to radians */
double degrees;
{
        do {
            degrees = degrees <  360.0 ? degrees : degrees - 360.0;
        } while ( degrees > 360 );
        do {
            degrees = degrees < -360.0 ? degrees + 360.0 : degrees;
        } while ( degrees < -360 );
        return ( degrees * 0.01745329 );
}
```

## rad2deg

## ( radians )

*Description:*   This is the "flip side" of the preceding function. It converts from radians to degrees. Radians are inherently floating-point values, and because of the precision possible with computers, the degrees returned by this function are also double. It is useful chiefly to convert computed results for output.

*Parameters:*   radians is a double.

*Type of Value Returned:*   double representing the equivalent of radians in degrees.

*Other Functions Called:*   None.

*Remarks:*   Unlike deg2rad, this function does not limit its result to plus or minus 360 degrees. Consequently, in the unlikely event that radians is greater in absolute value than 6.2831853, the result will also have an absolute value greater than 360.

```
double rad2deg ( radians )        /* radians to degrees */
double radians;
{
    return ( radians / 0.01745329 );
}
```

# Coordinate group

## distance

### ( x1, y1, x2, y2 )

*Description:* Using the standard distance formula, this function calculates the distance between two Cartesian points specified as usual with *x1, y1* and *x2, y2*. The parameters, incidentally, must be floats or doubles, even if specified as literal numbers. It won't do to call the function with

> d = distance ( 5, 7, 9, 11 )

since the literals are integers; you must code such a call as

> d = distance ( 5.0, 7.0, 9.0, 11.0 )

to coerce the compiler into making the literals floats as required by the function's heading. Naturally, you can also pass variables as parameters, providing they're doubles or floats.

*Parameters:*

> x1, y1 are the coordinates of one point, in type double.
> x2, y2 are the coordinates of the other point, also doubles (both sets may also be floats).

*Type of Value Returned:* double.

*Other Functions Called:* None.

```
double distance ( x1, y1, x2, y2 )      /* distance between two */
double x1, y1, x2, y2;                   /* points on a graph */
{
    double    sqrt (), x, y;

        x = ( x2 - x1 ) * ( x2 - x1 );
        y = ( y2 - y1 ) * ( y2 - y1 );
        return ( sqrt ( x + y ));
}
```

## mid__pt

## (x1, y1, x2, y2, results )

***Description:*** Given the coordinates of two end points on a line seg-
ment, this function finds the coordinates of the point exactly midway
between them. It's useful chiefly in applications that need to determine
the position of a bisector. The cir__ctr function given below, which
finds the center of a circle, demonstrates such an application.

***Parameters:***

> x1, y1 are the coordinates of one end point on the line segment, of
> type double.
> x2, y2 are the coordinates of the other point.
> results is a two-element array of double in which the function
> places its results. On return, the first element contains the *x* coor-
> dinate of the midpoint, the second element its *y* coordinate.

***Type of Value Returned:*** None (carried in results array).

***Other Functions Called:*** None.

```
mid_pt ( x1, y1, x2, y2, r )            /* midpoint of a line */
double x1, y1, x2, y2, r [];
{
    r [ 0 ] = x1 + (( x2 - x1 ) / 2.0 ),
    r [ 1 ] = y1 + (( y2 - y1 ) / 2.0 );
}
```

# Circle group

As you might have guessed by now, I've studied a lot of mathematics. Through it all, one of the things I've never been able to keep straight is which formulas—memorized in childhood—to use for the area and circumference of a circle. I'm not alone in that; people much better educated in math than I have asked me which is which. As a result, though it might seem a bit elementary, I've included those equations as the first two functions in this section; now we don't have to struggle to remember any more. The other two functions deal with attributes of spheres, the first cousins of circles.

## circum

**( radius )**

*Description:*   This function returns the circumference of a circle based on its radius. Both the radius and the returned circumference are doubles.

*Parameters:*   radius is a double.

*Type of Value Returned:*   double.

*Other Functions Called:*   None.

```
double circum ( radius )        /* circumference of a circle */
double radius;
{
    return ( 3.1415927 * 2.0 * radius );
}
```

## cir_area

## ( radius )

*Description:* As its name suggests, this function returns the area of a circle.

*Parameters:* radius is a double.

*Type of Value Returned:* double.

*Other Functions Called:* None.

```
double cir_area ( radius )       /* area of a circle */
double radius;
{
    return ( 3.1415927 * radius * radius );
}
```

# cir__ctr

## (x1, y1, x2, y2, x3, y3, result )

***Description:*** One of the trickiest pieces of programming in this book, cir__ctr is based on the well-established mathematical principle that any circle can be defined from the coordinates of three points on its circumference; if the circle passes through those points, it has only one possible center. The function takes the three points, computes the center, and returns the center coordinates in the result array, in which the first element is the center's *x* and the second is its *y*.

What makes this function so slick is the way it utilizes—and in the case of slope, fools—other functions defined in the chapter on algebra into solving the problem as a pair of linear equations in two unknowns. First it sorts the coordinate pairs to avoid the problems associated with perfectly vertical or horizontal lines, and then it finds the midpoints of the two lines described by the three points. By rearranging the parameters, it has slope compute the primes of the lines, which are the slopes of the perpendicular bisectors. It then works the *y*-intercept algorithm backwards in order to find where the bisectors, passing through the midpoints, intersect the *y* axis, thus providing a second pair of coordinates for each bisector. These then become pairs of coordinate sets, which l__sle resolves into standard linear equations whose coefficients are then fed to the sle2 function to find where the bisectors cross. This point is the center of the circle. The cir__ctr function returns this array to the calling program so that it can extract them as the *x* and *y* coordinates of the center.

***Parameters:***

> x1, y1 are the coordinates of one point on the circumference. All coordinates in this function are doubles.
> x2, y2 are the coordinates of a second point.
> x3, y3 are the coordinates of a third point.
> cc is an array of double having at least two elements, where the function will place the coordinates of the circle's center. The *x* is in cc [ 0 ], the *y* in cc [ 1 ].

***Type of Value Returned:*** An integer, where 0 means the set of three points does not describe a circle (they are in a straight line), and a nonzero value (nominally 1) means the function has successfully determined the circle's center.

***Other Functions Called:*** mid_pt, slope, l_sfe, sle2.

***Remarks:*** Note that a "zero" coordinate passed as a literal number must be in the format "0.0" and not simply "0," or else the parameter will be misinterpreted as an integer, causing the function to return incorrect results.

Note that the radius of the circle can be found by using the `distance` function with the center coordinates and those of any point on the circumference.

```
int cir_ctr ( x1, y1, x2, y2, x3, y3, cc )      /* find center of circle */
double x1, y1, x2, y2, x3, y3, cc [];           /*   from three points   */
{
    double    m1 [ 2 ] , m2 [ 2 ], c1 [ 3 ], c2 [ 3 ],
              sp1, sp2, slope (), yi1, yi2, tx, ty;

        if ( x1 == x2 ) {
            tx = x1;      ty = y1;
            x1 = x3;      y1 = y3;
            x3 = tx;      y3 = ty;
        }
        if ( x2 == x3 ) {
            tx = x1;      ty = y1;
            x1 = x2;      y1 = y2;
            x2 = tx;      y2 = ty;
        }
        if ( y1 == y2 ) {
            tx = x1;      ty = y1;
            x1 = x3;      y1 = y3;
            x3 - tx;      y3 = ty;
        }
        if ( y2 == y3 ) {
            tx = x1;      ty = y1,
            x1 = x2;      y1 = y2;
            x2 = tx;      y2 = ty;
        }
        mid_pt ( x1, y1, x2, y2, m1 );
        mid_pt ( x2, y2, x3, y3, m2 );    /* midpoints of two lines */
        if ( x2 == x3 && y1 == y3 ) {     /* lines at right angles */
            cc [ 0 ] = m1 [ 0 ];
            cc [ 1 ] = m1 [ 1 ];
            return ( 1 );
        }
        sp1 = slope ( y2, x1, y1, x2 );
        sp2 = slope ( y2, x3, y3, x2 );        /* slopes of bisectors */
        yi1 = m1 [ 0 ] * ( -sp1 ) + m1 [ 1 ];
        yi2 = m2 [ 0 ] * ( -sp2 ) + m2 [ 1 ];  /* y-ints of bisects */
        l_sfe ( m1 [ 0 ], m1 [ 1 ], 0.0, yi1, c1 );
        l_sfe ( m2 [ 0 ], m2 [ 1 ], 0.0, yi2, c2 ); /* coefficients */
        if ( sle2 ( c1, c2, cc ) == 0 )
            return ( 0 );                       /* if no solution */
        else
            return ( 1 );                  /* center coords in cc array */
}
```

## sph_area

## ( radius )

**Description:**  Computes and returns the area of a sphere based upon its radius.

**Parameters:**  radius is a double.

**Type of Value Returned:**  double.

**Other Functions Called:**  None.

```
double sph_area ( radius )      /* surface area of a sphere */
double radius;
{
    return ( 3.1415927 * 4.0 * radius * radius );
}
```

## sph__vol

## ( radius )

*Description:*  Returns the volume of a sphere.

*Parameters:*  radius is a double.

*Type of Value Returned:*  double.

*Other Functions Called:*  None.

---

```c
double sph_vol ( radius )      /* volume of a sphere */
double radius;
{
    double   r_cubed;

        r_cubed = radius * radius * radius;
        return ( 4.0 / 3.0 * r_cubed * 3.1415927 );
}
```

---

# Triangle group

In this section we deal with a number of aspects of triangles, one of the basic figures of geometry and the foundation for work involving curves, circles, and other shapes. The functions whose names begin with **rt** strictly concern right triangles, while those beginning with **t** have to do with irregular triangles (those not necessarily possessing a right angle).

The **t** functions utilize trigonometric and other transcendental functions that usually come with C products' standard libraries. Some variations, however, exist from one implementation to another. Before using the **t** functions, read the discussion at the start of the Trigonometric group below, so that you can check your compiler for compatibility.

## rt_area

## ( a, b )

**Description:**   Returns the area of a right triangle, given the two sides adjacent to the right angle.

**Parameters:**   a and b are the lengths of the two sides, given as numerics of type double.

**Type of Value Returned:**   double.

**Other Functions Called:**   None.

**Remarks:**   As in the algebra chapter (Chapter 5), make sure your compiler uses fabs in the standard library to return the absolute value of a floating-point number.

```
double rt_area ( a, b )      /* area of right triangle
                                   given two sides  */
double  a, b;
{
    double   fabs ();

       return ( fabs (( a * b ) / 2.0 ));
}
```

## rt__hyp

## ( a, b )

*Description:* Using the old faithful Pythagorean theorem, this function calculates and returns the length of the hypoteneuse of a right triangle based on the lengths of the other two sides.

*Parameters:* a and b are doubles giving the lengths of the two sides adjacent to the right angle.

*Type of Value Returned:* double.

*Other Functions Called:* None.

---

```
double rt_hyp ( a, b )          /* hypoteneuse of rt triangle */
double   a, b;
{
    double   sqrt ();

        return ( sqrt (( a * a ) + ( b * b )));
}
```

---

# rt__side

## ( hypoteneuse, side )

*Description:* Working the Pythagorean theorem backwards, this function finds the length of one of the sides of a right triangle, given the hypoteneuse and the other side.

*Parameters:* hypoteneuse and side are lengths expressed as doubles.

*Type of Value Returned:* double.

*Other Functions Called:* None.

```
double rt_side ( hyp, side )      /* find third side of right
                                     triangle, given hyp and side */
double hyp, side;
{
    double    sqrt ();

        return ( sqrt (( hyp * hyp ) - ( side * side )));
}
```

## t__2sia

**( side a, side b, angle c, results )**

***Description:*** Given the lengths of two sides and the measure of their included angle (in radians), this function solves any triangle for its remaining side and two remaining angles. The solutions are returned in the results array as follows:

results [ 0 ] = side $c$
results [ 1 ] = angle $a$ (in radians)
results [ 2 ] = angle $b$ (in radians)

The name of this function is an abbreviation for "Triangle: 2 Sides, Included Angle."

***Parameters:***

side a and side b are the lengths of two sides of the triangle, expressed as doubles.
angle c is a double, giving the measure in radians of the angle between the two sides given.
results is an array of three doubles where the function returns its results as described above.

***Type of Value Returned:*** None (modifies results array).

***Other Functions Called:*** None.

```
t_2sia ( side_a, side_b, angle_c, results )
double   side_a, side_b, angle_c, results [];
{
            /* triangle with two sides, included angle */

    double   side_c, angle_a, angle_b, cos (), atan (), sqrt (),
             bs, bc, pi = 3.1415927;

        angle_c = ( angle_c > pi ) ? ( pi * 2 - angle_c ) : angle_c;
        side_c = ( side_a * side_a ) + ( side_b * side_b ) -
                  2 * ( side_a * side_b * cos ( angle_c ));
        side_c = sqrt ( side_c );
        bc = (( side_c * side_c ) + ( side_a * side_a ) -
             ( side_b * side_b )) / ( 2 * side_a * side_c );
        bs = sqrt ( 1 - ( bc * bc ));
        angle_b = atan ( bs / bc );
        angle_b = ( angle_b < 0 ) ? angle_b + pi : angle_b;
        angle_a = pi - ( angle_b + angle_c );
        results [ 0 ] = side_c;
        results [ 1 ] = angle_a;
        results [ 2 ] = angle_b;
}
```

## t__2ais

### ( angle a, angle b, side c, results )

***Description:*** Given the measures (in radians) of two angles and the length of their included side, this function solves any triangle for its remaining angle and two remaining sides. The solutions are returned in the results array as follows:

> results [ Ø ] = angle *c* (in radians)
> results [ 1 ] = side *a*
> results [ 2 ] = side *b*

The name of this function is an abbreviation for "Triangle: 2 Angles, Included Side."

***Parameters:***

> angle a and angle b are doubles, giving the measure in radians of two angles.
> side c is the length of the side between the two angles given.
> results is an array of three doubles where the function returns its results as described above.

***Type of Value Returned:*** None (modifies results array).

***Other Functions Called:*** None.

```
t_2ais ( angle_a, angle_b, side_c, results )
double   angle_a, angle_b, side_c, results [];
{
        /* two angles, included side */

    double   angle_c, side_a, side_b, exp (), log (),
             sin (), pi = 3.1415927;

        angle_a = ( angle_a > pi ) ? ( pi * 2 - angle_a ) : angle_a;
        angle_b = ( angle_b > pi ) ? ( pi * 2 - angle_b ) : angle_b;
        angle_c = pi - ( angle_a + angle_b );
        side_a = exp ( log ( side_c ) - log ( sin ( angle_c )) +
                 log ( sin ( angle_a )));
        side_b = exp ( log ( side_c ) - log ( sin ( angle_c )) +
                 log ( sin ( angle_b )));
        results [ 0 ] = angle_c;
        results [ 1 ] = side_a;
        results [ 2 ] = side_b;
}
```

## t__3s

**( side a, side b, side c, results )**

*Description:* The name of this function stands for "Triangle: 3 Sides." As you might suppose, it finds the measures of the three angles opposing the sides whose lengths are given. It solves any form of triangle, returning the angles (in radians) as follows:

results [ 0 ] = angle a (opposite side a)
results [ 1 ] = angle b (opposite side b)
results [ 2 ] = angle c (opposite side c)

*Parameters:*

side a, side b, and side c are the lengths of the three sides of a triangle, of type double.

results is an array of at least three doubles where the function returns the angles as described above.

*Type of Value Returned:* None (modifies results).

*Other Functions Called:* None.

```
t_3s ( side_a, side_b, side_c, results )
double side_a, side_b, side_c, results [];
{
        /* three sides given */

    double   angle_a, angle_b, angle_c, sqrt (), atan (),
             sa2, sb2, sc2, as, bs, bc, pi = 3.1415927;

        sa2 = side_a * side_a;
        sb2 = side_b * side_b;
        sc2 = side_c * side_c;
        angle_c = ( sb2 + sc2 - sa2 ) / ( 2 * side_b * side_c );
        as = sqrt ( 1 - ( angle_c * angle_c ));
        angle_a = atan ( as / angle_c );
        angle_a = ( angle_a < 0 ) ? ( pi + angle_a ) : angle_a;
        bc = ( sc2 + sa2 - sb2 ) / ( 2 * side_a * side_c );
        bs = sqrt ( 1 - ( bc * bc ));
        angle_b = atan ( bs / bc );
        angle_b = ( angle_b < 0 ) ? ( pi + angle_b ) : angle_b;
        angle_c = pi - ( angle_a + angle_b );
        results [ 0 ] = angle_a;
        results [ 1 ] = angle_b;
        results [ 2 ] = angle_c;
}
```

# Trigonometric group

This section presents a number of extended trigonometric functions. By "extended," I refer to things that go beyond the normal sine and cosine, which are the basic functions of all trig, since most other functions derive from them in various ways. In order for the functions given below to work, your compiler must have, at minimum, the standard-library functions sin, cos, atan (or atn), log (or ln), and exp, which must directly return values that are either floats or doubles.

  You should take special care with the logarithm and antilog functions. In this book, we use log to derive a logarithm and exp to convert logs back into natural numbers. It's not so with all compilers. Some use ln instead of log, or have both, and in that case you must be sure to match the base of the log with the base of exp; if exp is to the base $e$, then use the logarithm function that is also to the base $e$. This might mean you have to substitute ln for log anywhere you encounter a reference to a logarithm in the listings. An #include file with appropriate macros will solve this problem.

  Another note of caution has to do with the name of the arctan function, which returns the angle (in radians) of a tangent. Most implementations of C have this function as part of the standard library, but the name varies. In some, it is atan, in others atn, and perhaps some others use arctan. Because my compiler uses atan, that's what it's called here; you should check your compiler's documentation to find the correct name before you type these functions, and substitute if necessary.

  Without exception, these trig functions work with radians, an inevitable circumstance in programming languages (see the discussion accompanying deg2rad above). It will, as a result, usually be necessary to use the deg2rad and rad2deg functions to convert between the normal degrees and the radians required here.

  As with certain other types of subprograms in this book, you may find you have little or no need for some of these extended trig functions, in which case there's no point in including them in your library. They'll still be here if you have a requirement for them later.

**tan**

## ( radians )

*Description:* Most compilers, but not all, come with **tan** as a standard library function. For those that don't, this function is given here, since it is important in trigonometry.

*Parameters:* radians is the angle in radians.

*Type of Value Returned:* double.

*Other Functions Called:* None (standard library for sin and cos).

```
double tan ( radians )    /* tangent of angle in radians */
double radians;
{
    double    sin (), cos ();

        return ( sin ( radians ) / cos ( radians ));
}
```

## cot

**( radians )**

*Description:*   Returns the cotangent of the angle.

*Parameters:*   radians is the angle.

*Type of Value Returned:*   double.

*Other Functions Called:*   Standard library.

```
double cot ( radians )    /* cotangent of angle in radians */
double radians;
{
    double    sin (), cos ();

        return ( cos ( radians ) / sin ( radians ));
}
```

## csc

## ( radians )

*Description:* Returns the cosecant of the angle in radians.

*Parameters:* radians is the angle.

*Type of Value Returned:* double.

*Other Functions Called:* Standard library.

```
double csc ( radians )    /* cosecant of angle in radians */
double radians;
{
    double    sin ();

        return ( 1 / sin ( radians ));
}
```

## sec

## ( radians )

*Description:*  Returns the secant of the angle in radians.

*Parameters:*  radians is the angle.

*Type of Value Returned:*  double.

*Other Functions Called:*  Standard library.

```
double sec ( radians )    /* secant of angle in radians */
double radians;
{
    double    cos ();

        return ( 1 / cos ( radians ));
}
```

## sinh

## ( radians )

*Description:* Returns the hyperbolic sine of the angle in radians.

*Parameters:* radians is the angle as a double.

*Type of Value Returned:* double.

*Other Functions Called:* None.

```
double  sinh ( radians )           /* hyperbolic sine */
double  radians;
{
    double    exp ();

        return (( exp ( radians ) - exp ( -radians )) / 2.0 );
}
```

**cosh**

## ( radians )

*Description:*   Returns the hyperbolic cosine of the angle in radians.

*Parameters:*   radians is the angle as a double.

*Type of Value Returned:*   double.

*Other Functions Called:*   None

```
double  cosh ( radians )          /* hyperbolic cosine */
double  radians;
{
    double    exp ();

        return (( exp ( radians ) + exp ( -radians )) / 2.0 );
}
```

## tanh

## ( radians )

**Description:** Returns the hyperbolic tangent of the angle in radians.

**Parameters:** radians is the angle as a double.

**Type of Value Returned:** double.

**Other Functions Called:** None

```
double   tanh ( radians )          /* hyperbolic tangent */
double   radians;
{
    double    exp (), mr;

        mr = exp ( -radians );
        return (( mr / exp ( radians ) + mr ) * 2.0 + 1.0 );
}
```

# ( radians )

*Description:*   Returns the hyperbolic secant of the angle in radians.

*Parameters:*   radians is the angle as a double.

*Type of Value Returned:*   double.

*Other Functions Called:*   None

```
double   sech ( radians )          /* hyperbolic secant */
double   radians;
{
    double    exp ();

        return ( 2.0 / ( exp ( radians ) + exp ( -radians )));
}
```

**csch**

## ( radians )

*Description:*  Returns the hyperbolic cosecant of the angle in radians.

*Parameters:*  radians is the angle as a double.

*Type of Value Returned:*  double.

*Other Functions Called:*  None

---

```
double  csch ( radians )          /* hyperbolic cosecant */
double  radians;
{
    double    exp ();

        return ( 2.0 / ( exp ( radians ) - exp ( -radians )));
}
```

---

## ( radians )

*Description:*   Returns the hyperbolic cotangent of the angle in radians.

*Parameters:*   radians is the angle as a double.

*Type of Value Returned:*   double.

*Other Functions Called:*   None

---

```
double   coth ( radians )          /* hyperbolic cotangent */
double   radians;
{
    double    exp (), mr;

        mr = exp ( -radians );
        return (( mr / exp ( radians ) - mr ) * 2.0 + 1.0 );
}
```

---

## arcsin

## ( sine )

*Description:*  Returns the angle in radians of a sine.

*Parameters:*  sine is the sine whose angle is to be found. It is a double.

*Type of Value Returned:*  double.

*Other Functions Called:*  Standard library.

---

```
double arcsin ( sine )          /* inverse sine */
double sine;
{
    double    atan (), sqrt ();

        return ( atan ( sine / sqrt ( -sine * sine + 1 )));
}
```

---

## arccos

### ( cosine )

*Description:*  Returns the angle in radians of a cosine.

*Parameters:*  cosine is the cosine whose angle is to be found. It is a double.

*Type of Value Returned:*  double.

*Other Functions Called:*  Standard library.

```
double arccos ( cosine )          /* inverse cosine */
double cosine;
{
    double    atan (), sqrt ();

        return ( -atan ( cosine / sqrt ( -cosine * cosine + 1 ))
            + 1.5708);
}
```

# CHAPTER **7**

# FINANCIAL PROGRAMMING FUNCTIONS

*F*inancial applications are the bread and butter of computer programming. It is, after all, business that makes the most use of computers, and business is primarily concerned with making money, and computers do a better job of wending through the complexities of finance than people can.

The most challenging aspect of finance has to do with the time value of money, and that's what we concentrate on in this chapter. Bookkeeping applications are relatively simple—mainly addition and subtraction—but computations involving interest applied over time are difficult and lend themselves extremely well to "computerization." In all the years I spent as a data-processing manager in a large bank, I never encountered a loan officer who didn't have a calculator, reams of interest tables, crib sheets for the formulas, and a computer terminal by his or her side; they usually did their computations by hand, then made sure they were right by asking the computer (and I still wonder why they didn't just turn to the computer and save all that extra work).

The functions in this chapter "remember" the formulas on those crib sheets, and they do the necessary calculations faster than it takes to find and press just one key on a calculator. These functions are, to a great degree, what computers are about.

They are not the sole province, however, of the corporate world. Hobbyists and home computer users can utilize them to advantage as well in figuring loan payments, computing interest, planning investments, and for other financial purposes. They harness the computer to the load it is best suited to draw: complex calculations that lead to useful results too difficult (or at least too time-consuming) for most of us—including bank loan-officers—to figure out with confidence by hand.

Without exception, these functions deal with values of type double, since interest and finance in general concern themselves with pennies and percentages carried out to numerous decimal places. The same cautions apply as in earlier chapters, notably the one on the algebraic functions (Chapter 5), regarding the standardization of the C compiler where it comes to floating-point operations.

This chapter includes the following functions:

| | |
|---|---|
| pwf | Factor for present worth of a future amount, given continuous compounding. |
| pwfa | Present worth of a future amount. |
| capa | Continuous annuity from a present amount. |
| pwca | Present worth of a continuous annuity. |
| fwf | Factor for future worth of a present amount, given continuous compounding. |
| fwpa | Future worth of a present amount. |
| cafa | Continuous annuity for a future amount. |
| fwca | Future worth of a continuous annuity. |
| mo_pmt | Monthly payment for a loan. |

## ( rate, years)

***Description:*** The `pwf` function returns a `double` that is the factor (multiplier) for the present worth of a continuously compounding annuity. This factor is the basis for predicting the value, in today's dollars, of a desired future amount, given a steady `rate` of interest over some number of `years`. It is useful both on its own and as a called calculation for other functions presented later in the chapter (see `pwfa` in the following section for a working example).

Note that the `rate` of interest must be a `double`, but that it can be either a whole number with an optional fraction or a fractional number, and the function will adjust its value to a true percentage interest rate. For example, if the stated interest rate is 11.5 percent, you can pass `rate` as 11.5 or as Ø.115; if 11.5, the second processing statement of the function converts it to Ø.115. The rationale here is to eliminate any ambiguity on the user's part as to which format is required; it is unlikely that an interest rate of greater than 100 percent will ever apply to any loan advanced by organizations other than the Mafia, even in times of rampant inflation.

***Parameters:***

   `rate` is the fixed annual interest rate expressed as a `double`.
   `years` is the number of years, in the form of a `double`, over which
      the present worth is computed (a month is Ø.Ø833333 of a year
      and is an allowable unit of time in this function).

***Type of Value Returned:*** `double` (if less than Ø.Ø, it means that the function could not complete properly; otherwise, it returns the present-worth factor for the period and interest rate).

***Other Functions Called:*** `fpower`, standard library.

```
double  pwf ( rate, years )              /* present worth factor */
double  rate, years;      /* cont compounding, single amount  */
{
    double    ejn, j, log (), fpower ();

        if ( rate < 0.001 || years < 0.08 )
            return ( -1.0 );                /* bad parm passed */
        rate = ( rate < 1 ) ? rate : rate / 100.0;
        ejn = fpower (( 1 + rate ), years );
        j = log ( 1 + rate ) / log ( 2.71828 );
        return (( ejn - 1.0 ) / ( j * ejn ));
}
```

## ( amount, rate, years )

*Description:*   The name of this function comes from the initials of the frequently used economic term Present Worth of a Future Amount. It assumes a single **amount** continuously compounded at a fixed **rate** of interest over some number of **years** (which may be a fractional number with Ø.Ø833333 being one month). The value it returns is the amount of money to be invested today to achieve that future amount. Because it calls the **pwf** function, an interest rate such as 11.5 percent can be expressed either as 11.5 or as Ø.115, and the function will adjust it appropriately.

*Parameters:*

amount is a double giving the future value.
rate is the percentage interest rate yielded by the investment.
years is a double showing the life of the investment.

*Type of Value Returned:*   double giving the present worth of the future amount.

*Other Functions Called:*   pwf.

*Remarks:*   Makes no provision for inflation.

```
double   pwfa ( amt, rate, years )    /* pres worth of future amt */
double   amt, rate, years;
{
    double    pwf (), n, nl;

        if (( n = pwf ( rate, years )) < 0.0 )
            return ( -1.0 );
        if ( years >= 1.0 )
            nl = pwf ( rate, years - 1.0 );
        else
            nl = 0;
        return ( amt * ( n - nl ));
}
```

**capa**

## ( rate, years )

*Description:*   The name capa stands for Continuous Annuity from a Present Amount. The proposition is this: If you have a certain amount on deposit at a fixed interest rate, how much can you withdraw in annual installments to have the fund last exactly so many years? The function returns a factor that is a double. Multiply it by the amount on deposit to determine the annuity.

*Parameters:*

    rate is the fixed annual interest rate expressed as a double.
    years is the number of years, in the form of a double, over which
        the annuity is computed (a month is 0.0833333 of a year and is an
        allowable unit of time in this function).

*Type of Value Returned:*   double (if less than 0.0, it means that the function could not complete properly; otherwise, it returns the annuity factor for the period and interest rate).

*Other Functions Called:*   fpower, standard library.

```
double   capa ( rate, years )   /* cont annuity from pres amt */
double   rate, years;
{
    double    ejn, j, log (), fpower ();

        if ( rate < 0.001 || years < 0.08 )
            return ( -1.0 );                  /* bad parm passed */
        rate = ( rate < 1 ) ? rate : rate / 100.0;
        ejn = fpower (( 1 + rate ), years );
        j = log ( 1 + rate ) / log ( 2.71828 );
        return (( j * ejn ) / ( ejn - 1.0 ));
}
```

**pwca**

## ( rate, years )

***Description:*** Present Worth of a Continuous Annuity: if you want an annuity of a certain amount that has to last exactly so many years, how much do you have to put on deposit at a fixed rate compounded continuously to achieve it? pwca returns a factor that is a double. Multiply it by the desired annuity to find the amount you must invest.

***Parameters:***

> rate is the fixed annual interest rate expressed as a double.
> years is the number of years, in the form of a double, over which
> the annuity is computed (a month is 0.0833333 of a year and is an
> allowable unit of time in this function).

***Type of Value Returned:*** double (if less than 0.0, it means that the function could not complete properly; otherwise, it returns the annuity factor for the period and interest rate).

***Other Functions Called:*** fpower, standard library.

```
double  pwca ( rate, years )   /* pres worth of cont annuity */
double  rate, years;
{
    double    ejn, j, log (), fpower ();

        if ( rate < 0.001 || years < 0.08 )
            return ( -1.0 );              /* bad parm passed */
        rate = ( rate < 1 ) ? rate : rate / 100.0;
        ejn = fpower (( 1 + rate ), years );
        j = log ( 1 + rate ) / log ( 2.71828 );
        return (( ejn - 1.0 ) / ( j * ejn ));
}
```

**fwf**

## ( rate, years )

*Description:*  The fwf function returns a double that is the factor (multiplier) for the future worth of a continuously compounding annuity. This factor is the basis for predicting the value of a present amount after some number of years, given a steady rate of interest. It is useful both on its own and as a called calculation for other functions presented later in the chapter (see fwpa in the following section for a working example).

Note that the rate of interest must be a double, but that it can be either a whole number with an optional fraction or a fractional number, and the function will adjust its value to a true percentage interest rate. For example, if the stated interest rate is 11.5 percent, you can pass rate as 11.5 or as Ø.115; if 11.5, the second processing statement of the function converts it to Ø.115. The rationale here is to eliminate any ambiguity on the user's part as to which format is required; it is unlikely that an interest rate of greater than 100 percent will ever prevail.

*Parameters:*

> rate is the fixed annual interest rate expressed as a double.
> years is the number of years, in the form of a double, over which
>   the present worth is computed (a month is Ø.Ø833333 of a year
>   and is an allowable unit of time in this function).

*Type of Value Returned:*  double (if less than Ø.Ø, it means that the function could not complete properly; otherwise, it returns the future-worth factor for the period and interest rate).

*Other Functions Called:*  fpower, standard library.

```
double  fwf ( rate, years )              /* future worth factor */
double  rate, years;      /* cont compounding, single amount   */
{
    double    ejn, j, log (), fpower ();

        if ( rate < 0.001 || years < 0.08 )
            return ( -1.0 );                /* bad parm passed */
        rate = ( rate < 1 ) ? rate : rate / 100.0;
        ejn = fpower (( 1 + rate ), years );
        j = log ( 1 + rate ) / log ( 2.71828 );
        return (( ejn - 1.0 ) / j );
}
```

**fwpa**

# ( amount, rate, years )

***Description:*** The name of this function comes from the initials of the economic term Future Worth of a Present Amount. It assumes a single amount continuously compounded at a fixed rate of interest over some number of years (which may be a fractional number with 0.0833333 being one month). The value it returns is the worth in dollars of the present amount at the end of the period. Because it calls the fwf function, an interest rate such as 11.5 percent can be expressed either as 11.5 or as 0.115, and the function will adjust it appropriately.

***Parameters:***

amount is a double giving the present value.
rate is the percentage interest rate yielded by the investment.
years is a double showing the life of the investment.

***Type of Value Returned:*** double giving the future worth of the present amount.

***Other Functions Called:*** fwf.

***Remarks:*** Makes no provision for inflation.

```
double  fwpa ( amt, rate, years )   /* future worth of pres amt */
double  amt, rate, years;
{
    double   fwf (), n, nl;

        if (( n = fwf ( rate, years )) < 0.0 )
            return ( -1.0 );
        if ( years >= 1.0 )
            nl = fwf ( rate, years - 1.0 );
        else
            nl = 0;
        return ( amt * ( n - nl ));
}
```

## cafa

## ( rate, years )

***Description:***   Continuous annuity for a future amount: if you want to have a certain amount after so many years, how much do you have to set aside annually at a fixed rate compounded continuously? The function returns a factor that you multiply by the desired future amount to find the annuity.

***Parameters:***

rate is the fixed annual interest rate expressed as a double.
years is the number of years, in the form of a double, over which the annuity is computed (a month is 0.0833333 of a year and is an allowable unit of time in this function).

***Type of Value Returned:***   double (if less than 0.0, it means that the function could not complete properly; otherwise, it returns the annuity factor for the period and interest rate).

***Other Functions Called:***   fpower, standard library.

```
double  cafa ( rate, years )   /* cont annuity for future amt */
double  rate, years;
{
    double    ejn, j, log (), fpower ();

        if ( rate < 0.001 || years < 0.08 )
            return ( -1.0 );                /* bad parm passed */
        rate = ( rate < 1 ) ? rate : rate / 100.0;
        ejn = fpower (( 1 + rate ), years );
        j = log ( 1 + rate ) / log ( 2.71828 );
        return ( j / ( ejn - 1.0 ));
}
```

## fwca

## ( rate, years )

*Description:*   Future Worth of a Continuous Annuity: if you are putting a regular amount each year into an account bearing a fixed interest rate continuously compounded, how much will the investment be worth after a certain number of years? The function returns a factor by which you multiply the annual installment to find the future worth.

*Parameters:*

rate is the fixed annual interest rate expressed as a double.
years is the number of years, in the form of a double, over which the annuity is computed (a month is 0.0833333 of a year and is an allowable unit of time in this function).

*Type of Value Returned:*   double (if less than 0.0, it means that the function could not complete properly; otherwise, it returns the annuity factor for the period and interest rate).

*Other Functions Called:*   fpower, standard library.

```
double   fwca ( rate, years )   /* future worth of cont annuity */
double   rate, years;
{
    double    ejn, j, log (), fpower ();

        if ( rate < 0.001 || years < 0.08 )
            return ( -1.0 );                /* bad parm passed */
        rate = ( rate < 1 ) ? rate : rate / 100.0;
        ejn = fpower (( 1 + rate ), years );
        j = log ( 1 + rate ) / log ( 2.71828 );
        return (( ejn - 1.0 ) / j );
}
```

## ( amount, rate, number )

*Description:* Given the principal amount of the loan, the annual percentage interest rate, and the number of monthly payments, this function returns the dollar amount of each monthly installment. It, like the other functions in this chapter, assumes continuous compounding.

*Parameters:*

amount is a double giving the principal amount of the loan.
rate is a double expressing the effective annual interest rate charged.
number is an integer specifying the number of monthly installments in the repayment period.

*Type of Value Returned:* double (a negative amount if the function encountered unusable parameters; otherwise, it is the monthly payment for the loan terms given).

*Other Functions Called:* capa.

```
double mo_pmt ( amount, rate, n )   /* monthly payment for loan */
double   amount, rate;              /* w/continuous compounding */
int      n;
{
    double    pmts, factor, capa ();

        rate = ( rate > 1.0 ) ? ( rate / 1200.0 ) : ( rate / 12.0 );
        pmts = ( double ) ( n );
        if (( factor = capa ( rate, pmts )) < 0.0 )
            return ( factor );
        return ( amount * factor );
}
```

# CHAPTER **8**

# HANDY UTILITIES

*I*t seems more appropriate to call the functions in this chapter "handy" than the more amorphous "miscellaneous." The latter term suggests afterthoughts of little value, thrown in to justify a certain price. Such isn't the case here; these are all useful tools, but they're somewhat heterogeneous and don't belong to some grander category that merits a chapter all its own.

This chapter is unusual in that it not only brings together uncategorized functions, but also includes complete programs that furnish useful services for computer users.

In the following list of contents, function names are given in boldface lowercase letters and complete program names in uppercase boldface.

| | |
|---|---|
| cal__1m | Day of the week for the first day of any month. |
| CALENDAR | Perpetual calendar program. |
| cal__dow | Day of the week for any date after 1900. |
| SETFK | Sets function keys to generate commands. |
| COLLECT | A file insertion program. |
| HEXDUMP | Hexadecimal dump of a file. |
| bar | Vertical 3-dimensional bar for bar graphs. |

**cal_lm**

## ( month, year )

*Description:* cal_lm is admittedly a cryptic name, a result of the savagely terse abbreviations imposed by eight-character filenames and linkage editors. It is meant to suggest a calendar program that returns the first day of any month of any year. The idea is that your program furnishes the month (as a number from 1 through 12 for January through December) and the year (e.g., 1986), and the function replies with a digit telling what day of the week was the first of the month. The digits are Ø = Sunday, 1 = Monday, . . . , 6 = Saturday. This function is useful for constructing calendars, as the CALENDAR program given next demonstrates.

The cal_lm function provides a perpetual calendar for any year from 1901 onward. If you pass a year parameter lower in numeric value than 19Ø1, or an invalid month number such as 13 or Ø, the function returns the digit 7 as an error indicator. It never returns a value less than Ø. You can thus check for an error with a statement sequence such as:

```
if (( day1 = cal_lm ( m, y )) < 7
  ( result is valid )
else
  ( an error has occurred )
```

*Parameters:*

> month is an integer from 1 through 12 giving the ordinal of the month.
> year is an integer with a value of 19Ø1 or greater, giving the year.

*Type of Value Returned:* Integer (Ø = Sunday, . . ., 6 = Saturday).

*Other Functions Called:* None.

```c
int cal_1m ( mo, yr )    /* first day of any month after 1900 */
int mo, yr;
{
    int     d, nd, mt [] = {   0,  31,  59,  90, 120, 151,
                             181, 212, 243, 273, 304, 334 };

        if ( yr < 1901 || mo < 1 || mo > 12 )
            return ( 7 );        /* parm error */
        d = yr - 1901;
        nd = d * 365;
        nd += (( d / 4 ) - ( d / 100 ) + ( d / 400 ))
                + mt [ mo - 1 ];
        if (( yr % 4 ) == 0 && mo > 2 )
            nd++;
        return (( nd + 2 ) % 7 );
}
```

## CALENDAR

*Description:*   This is a complete program that displays on the screen the calendar for any month from January 1901 onward. It's a very useful utility for anyone who needs to plan ahead or look back in time during this century. It will look ahead to any year through 32767, which is probably longer than anyone ever plans in advance anyway.

*Operation:*   Type the program name (**CALENDAR**): The program identifies itself and asks for

### Month, year. . .

Type the month number (1 for January, 2 for February, etc.), a comma, and the year. For example, to get the calendar for June 1986, the entry is

### 6, 1986

After the last digit, press the ENTER key. The computer will immediately display the calendar for that month, after which the program will end. If you type an invalid month (outside the range 1, . . ., 12) or a year prior to 1901, the program replies

### ERROR IN DATE

and ends without further action.

*Functions Called:*   cal__lm.

```
#include <stdio.h>       /* perpetual calendar from 1901 onward */
main ()
{
    int mo, year, atoi(), day, c, s, cal_lm();
    static  dpm [] = { 31, 28, 31, 30, 31, 30,
                       31, 31, 30, 31, 30, 31 };
    char    m [ 3 ], y [ 5 ];
    static char *n [] = { "January", "February", "March", "April",
            "May", "June", "July", "August", "September",
            "October", "November", "December" };

        puts ( "\nPerpetual calendar from 1901 onward:\n\n" );
        puts ( "\nMonth, year... " );
        scanf ( "%s, %s", m, y );
        mo = atoi ( m );
        year = atoi ( y );
```

```
          if (( day = cal_lm ( mo, year )) > 6 ) {
              puts  ( "\nERROR IN DATE" );
              exit ( 1 );
          }
          mo--;
          printf ( "\n\nCalendar for %s, %d:", n [ mo ], year );
          puts ( "\n  Su  Mo  Tu  We  Th  Fr  Sa" );
          puts ( "\n  --  --  --  --  --  --  --\n" );
          s = 0;
          if ( day > 0 )
              for ( s = 0; s < day; s++ );
                  puts ( "    " );    /* four cols per date */
          c = s;
          day = 1;
          do {
              printf ( "%4d", day++ );
              if ( ++c > 6 ) {
                  putchar ( '\n' );
                  c = 0;
              }
          } while ( day <= dpm [ mo ] );
          if ( mo == 1 && ( year % 4 ) == 0 )
              if (( year % 100 ) != 0 || ( year % 400 ) == 0 )
                  printf ( "%4d", day );  /* Feb 29 */
          puts ( "\n\n\n" );
      }
```

---

## cal__dow

### ( month, date, year )

***Description:*** This function resembles cal__1m, except that instead of returning the first day of the week of the specified month, it returns the day of the week of any given date after January 1, 1901. The days of the week are Ø = Sunday, 1 = Monday, etc., through 6 = Saturday. For example, if you call this function for July 17, 1941 with

    day = cal__dow ( 7, 17, 1941 )

it returns the integer 4, signifying a Thursday.

***Parameters:***

> month is an integer or integer variable in the range 1–12.
> date is a valid date of the month given, again as an integer.
> year is an integer expressing any year from 1901 onward through the year 32767.

***Type of Value Returned:*** Integer, where Ø = Sunday and the rest of the days of the week follow in progression.

***Other Functions Called:*** None.

***Remarks:*** If the month is outside the normal range 1–12, the date is less than 1 or greater than 31, or the year is earlier than 1901, the function returns 7 as an error code. Note that it does not check for the appropriate number of days per month; February 31 is a valid date, for example, but the function translates it into a March date and adjusts for leap years in the process (March 3 or 4, depending on the year).

```
int cal_dow ( mo, date, yr )      /* day of the week for any */
int mo, yr;                       /*    date after 1/1/1901   */
{
    int     d, nd;
    static  mt [] = {   0,   31,   59,   90, 120, 151,
                      181, 212, 243, 273, 304, 334 };

        if ( yr < 1091 || mo < 1 || mo > 12 ||
              date < 1 || date > 31 )
            return ( 7 );          /* parm error */
        d = yr - 1901;
        nd = d * 365;
        nd += (( d / 4 ) - ( d / 100 ) + ( d / 400 )) +
              mt [ mo - 1 ] + date - 1;
        if (( yr % 4 ) == 0 && mo > 2 )
            nd++;
        return (( nd + 2 ) % 7 );
}
```

## ( optional command line )

*Description:*  This is a complete program that lets you set up function keys on the IBM PC and compatibles to generate macros, such as system commands and program names that include command line parameters. For example, you might want the F9 key, when pressed, to have the effect of "dir a:/w" which furnishes a wide listing of the directory for drive A:. The SETFK program gives you two ways to make the assignment to F9: interactively, or via the command line that starts the program.

To set function keys interactively, bring up the program by typing its name (SETFK) and pressing ENTER. The program then identifies itself and asks you to type the number of the function key. Using the example above of assigning "dir a:/w" to F9, you'd type 9 in response to this question. The program next asks for the command you want to assign to that key. Type the command exactly as you would if working at the DOS command level (with an A⟩ prompt), and don't put quotes around it. The program then asks for the number of another function key, repeating the process. You can go on assigning macros to as many function keys as necessary. When you have no more assignments to make, press ENTER in response to the function-key-number request. The program completes by reporting the macros and the keys to which it assigned them.

The alternative method of feeding parameters is via the command line. This lets you include **SETFK** in batch files such as AUTO-EXEC.BAT, so that it will automatically make function-key assignments without having to interact with it. The following command line assigns "dir a:/w" to F9 and "dir b:" to F10:

**setfk 9, dir a:/w, 1Ø, dir b:**

Note that the order of parameters is key number, macro, key number, macro. You can continue this sequence for as many keys as necessary. Also, if all the assignments won't fit on one command line, you can reexecute the program giving different sets of assignments each time. **SETFK** only affects already-existing assignments when you make a second assignment to the same key (set F1Ø, for example, to one command, then change F1Ø to another).

Function-key assignments made by **SETFK** remain in effect for as long as the computer is turned on, with one exception; if you run another program that "owns" the function keys, such as Lotus 1-2-3, Framework, or WordStar, that program will probably restore the function keys to their state at power-up time, thus removing the assignments made by **SETFK**. In that case, you'll have to rerun **SETFK** to reinstate your own function-key configuration.

*Parameters:*   Optional command line as described above.

*Type of Value Returned:*   None.

*Other Functions Called:*   `fkey`, standard library.

*Error handling:*   **SETFK** makes no attempt to validate the actual macro you assign to a key. It does evaluate the function key number and report on the screen when an invalid number is given via the interactive or command-line inputs, after which it moves on to the next key number and acts on it appropriately.

*Remarks:*   The ANSI.SYS device driver must be resident in memory to enable this program to operate, inasmuch as the `fkey` function communicates with ANSI.SYS. See the preface to the chapter on screen functions (Chapter 3) for more discussion.

    **SETFK** regards commas as delimiters between parameters. Thus, a macro being assigned to a key may not contain embedded commas, or the program will malfunction and not tell you why.

```
#include <stdio.h>

    /* assign command(s) to function key(s) on IBM PC */
        /* ANSI.SYS device driver must be resident */

    char    cmd [ 256 ];    /* global */
main ( argc, argv )
int     argc;
char    *argv [];
{
        if ( argc > 1 ) {
            mkcl ( argc, argv );
            parse ();
        } else {
            key_in ();
            parse ();
        }
}   /* ------------------------------------------------- */

mkcl ( n, cl )              /* assemble internal cmd line */
    int     n;              /* from program command line  */
```

```
char     *cl [];
{
    int      c, p;

        p = 0;
        while ( --n > 0 ) {
            c = strlen ( *++cl );
            strcpy ( &cmd [ p ], *cl );
            p += c;
            cmd [ p++ ] = ' ';
        }
        cmd [ --p ] = '\0';
}    /* ------------------------------------------- */

key_in ()                         /* interactive assignment */
{
    int      p, m, fkey;
    char     macro [ 80 ];

        p = 0;
        puts ( "\n\n\nFunction key assignment program:" );
        puts ( "\n-----------------------------" );
        do {
            puts ( "\n\nFunction key number (or press" );
            puts ( "\n  ENTER key to end program)... " );
            gets ( macro );
            if (( m = strlen ( macro )) > 0 ) {
                if (( fkey = atoi ( macro )) > 0 && fkey < 11 ) {
                    strcpy ( &cmd [ p ], macro );
                    strcpy ( &cmd [ p ], macro );
                    p += strlen ( macro );
                    cmd [ p++ ] = ',';
                } else
                    puts ( "\nInvalid function key" );
            }
        } while ( m > 0 );
        cmd [ --p ] = '\0';
}    /* ------------------------------------------- */

parse ()              /* act on command string */
{
    int      s, p, keyn;
    char     macro [ 80 ], num [ 6 ], c;

        s = 0;
        while ( cmd [ s ] != '\0' ) {
            p = 0;
            if ( cmd [ s ] == ',' )
                s++;
            while (( c = cmd [ s++ ] ) != ',' )
                num [ p++ ] = c;
```

```
        num [ p ] = '\0';
        p = 0;
        keyn = atoi ( num );
        if ( keyn > 0 && keyn < 11 ) {
            while ( cmd [ s ] == ' ' )
                s++;
            while (( c = cmd [ s++ ] ) != ',' && c != '\0' )
                macro [ p++ ] = c;
            macro [ p ] = '\0';
            fkey ( keyn, macro );
            printf ( "\nSet F%d for command %s", keyn, macro );
        } else {
            printf ( "\nInvalid key #%d in command line" );
            while (( c = cmd [ s ] ) != ',' && c != '\0' )
                s++;
        }
    }
}
```

# COLLECT D:FILENAME.EXT

***Description:*** This program is mentioned in the introduction to the book as one of the means available to you for assembling function libraries. It is, however, a general-purpose program useful for text processing and any other situations in which you need to combine the contents of two or more files into one. It is therefore a collector of files, hence its name.

The program goes through a text file looking for the keyword **%insert** at the left end of each line. The **%insert** directive must be followed by a space, then the name of a file to be "sucked in" at the point where **%insert** occurs. The **%inserted** filename should include a drive designator (if not, the program always looks on the A: drive, *not* on the default drive).

As an admittedly trivial example, suppose you have a file called FILE2.XYZ on the C: drive, whose contents read "THIS IS FROM FILE2," and you want to include these contents in a new file called SOMETHING.XYZ on the B: drive. The first thing you would do is to use an editor of some sort to create B:SOMETHING.XYZ. Where you expect the contents of C:FILE2.XYZ to appear, type the **%insert** directive. Thus SOMETHING, which we will call the source file, might read:

    This is something.
    %insert c:file2.xyz
    Something continues.

When you have finished editing the SOMETHING file, exit to the operating system, then type the command

**collect b:something.xyz**

The COLLECT program then runs. When it encounters the **%insert**, it goes to the C: drive and sticks the contents of the named file into the source file, so that afterwards, SOMETHING.XYZ reads:

    This is something.
    THIS IS FROM FILE2
    Something continues.

Note that the **%insert** directive has been replaced by the contents of the named file and no longer appears in the source file. It is as though the second line had been typed directly into SOMETHING.XYZ.

In "real-life" situations, of course, you would use COLLECT to bring longer files into the source file. In the case of assembling function libraries, you might decide to establish a library of hexadecimal conversion functions called D:HEXLIB.C, bringing together several individual subprograms on the B: drive. The initial HEXLIB file would consist entirely of %inserts:

```
%insert b:atox.c
%insert b:xtoa.c
%insert b:itox.c
%insert b:xtoi.c
```

To create the actual source library, type the command

**collect d:hexlib.c**

After the COLLECT program has completed, D:HEXLIB.C will contain the four subprograms, each of which is identical to the file from which it came. You can then compile HEXLIB to convert it into a linkable library.

Later, you might decide to add other functions to HEXLIB. All you need to do is edit the file to add the new %inserts at the appropriate places, then run COLLECT again.

The COLLECT program reports when it is inserting a file, and at the conclusion of the run it tells how many files it added to the source file; that is, how many %inserts it successfully processed.

When %insert points to a nonexistent file, the program beeps at you and reports an error. You are then given the option of continuing or quitting. If you quit, all work done so far on the source file is abandoned and the source file will be identical to what it contained before the abortive run of COLLECT. If you continue, the %insert that caused the trouble will remain in the source file where it was encountered, and COLLECT will run to normal completion. Any successful %inserts will have been replaced by the appropriate file contents. The rationale here is that you can then edit the source file to locate the troublesome %inserts and fix it.

COLLECT also reports other unrecoverable errors, most of which are self-explanatory. The "Unable to write to work file" error usually means that the disk is full. In any unrecoverable error, COLLECT abandons work already done on the source file and restores it to its original condition.

This is a handy program. I used it extensively in writing this book. It does not, by the way, utilize any of the functions presented in this book, but is instead "vanilla C code" using only the standard library, so that those who are just setting out to expand their libraries via this book can type it as their first program.

*Parameters:* Include the name of the file containing the %insert directive(s) on the command line. Only one filename is allowed on the command line per execution of COLLECT. A disk drive designator is recommended.

---

```
/* program COLLECT        K. Porter     1/28/85 */
#include <stdio.h>

        int             count;          /* global */

main ( argc, argv )
int     argc;
char    *argv [];
{
    int     in, out, p;
    char    buf [ 256 ], sf [ 15 ], tf [ 15 ];

        puts ( "\n\n\n\nCOLLECT -- A FILE INSERTION UTILITY\n\n" );
        if ( argc == 1 ) {
            puts ( "\nInclude source filename in command line\n" );
            exit ( 1 );
        } else {
            if ( argc > 2 ) {
                puts ( "\nOnly one source file allowed\n" );
                exit ( 1 );
            }
        }
        strcpy ( sf, argv [ 1 ] );                  /* source filename */
        if (( in = fopen ( sf, "r" )) == 0 ) {         /* open it */
            printf ( "\nCannot open source file %s\n", sf );
            exit ( 1 );
        }
        p = count = 0;
        if ( sf [ 1 ] == ':' ) {                  /* use same drive */
            tf [ p++ ] = sf [ 0 ];
            tf [ p++ ] = ':';
        }
        strcpy ( &tf [ p ], "SKLRGX.$$$" );            /* work file */
        if (( out = creat ( tf )) == -1 ) {
            puts ( "\nCannot create work file\n" );
            exit ( 1 );
        }
        while ( fgets ( buf, 255, in ) != 0 ) {    /* read */
            if ( buf [ 0 ] != '%' ) {
                if ( fputs ( buf, out ) == -1 )      /* copy */
                    fwerr ( in, out, tf );
```

```
            } else {
                if ( ckins ( buf ) == 0 ) {
                    insert ( buf, out, tf, in );
                    count++;
                } else
                    fputs ( buf, out );
            }
        }
        fclose ( in );                      /* close both files */
        fclose ( out );
        unlink ( sf );                      /* delete orig source */
        rename ( tf, sf );                  /* replace with workfile */
        printf ( "\n%d files inserted", count );
        puts ( "\nCOLLECT ended normally\n" );

        exit ( 0 );
}       /* ------------------------------------------------------- */

fwerr ( sd, fd, name )          /* error -- cannot write to workfile */
int        sd, fd;
char    name [];
{
    puts ( "\nError: Unable to write to work file" );
    abort ( sd, fd, name );
}       /* ------------------------------------------------------- */

int ckins ( line )              /* check line for '%insert' */
char    line [];
{
    int         i;
    char    cmp [ 7 ];

        strcpy ( cmp, "%insert" );
        for ( i = 0; i < 7; i++ ) {
            if ( line [ i ] != cmp [ i ] )
                return ( 1 );
        }
        return ( 0 );           /* match found */
}       /* ------------------------------------------------------- */

insert ( line, wp, tf, sp )             /* insert file */
char    line [], tf [];
int     wp, sp;
{
    int     ip, x, y;
    char    name [ 15 ], bfr [ 256 ];

        for ( x = 0; x < 15; x++ )
            name [ x ] = '\0';
        y = 7;
        while ( line [ y ] == ' ' )
            y++;
```

```
        strcpy ( name, &line [ y ] );              /* get filename */
        for ( x = 14; x > 0; x-- ) {               /* remove '\n'   */
            if ( name [ x ] == '\n' )
                name [ x ] = '\0';
        }
        if (( ip = fopen ( name, "r" )) == 0 ) {
            printf ( "\n\nError: Unable to open insert file %s", name );
            putchar ( 7 );                          /* beep */
            puts ( "\nContinue (y/n)? " );
            if ( tolower ( getchar () ) == 'y' ) {
                fputs ( line, wp );
                count--;
                return;
            } else
                abort ( wp, sp, tf );
        }
        printf ( "\n\nInserting %s", name );
        while (( x = fgets ( bfr, 255, ip )) != 0 ) {
            if ( fputs ( bfr, wp ) == -1 ) {
                puts ( "\nError: Unable to write to work file" );
                abort ( wp, sp, tf );
            }
        }
        fclose ( ip );
}    /* ------------------------------------------------------------ */

abort ( sf, wf, temp )           /* end job on error */
int    sf, wf;
char   temp [];
{
    fclose ( sf );
    fclose ( wf );
    unlink ( temp );
    puts ( "\nCOLLECT ended\n" );
    exit ( 1 );
}    /* ------------------------------------------------------------ */
```

# HEXDUMP D:FILENAME.EXT

***Description:*** This is both a useful utility and a demonstration of several functions presented throughout the book. It is written specifically for IBM and compatible machines. The HEXDUMP program allows you to inspect the contents of any file in detail, viewing it in both hexadecimal and ASCII according to the standard dump format discussed under the dump16 function in Chapter 2. It works in 256-byte blocks (16 lines by 16 bytes). Dumps such as this are invaluable in running troubles on files and figuring out if they are corrupted, for determining control bytes inserted into data, and other close scrutiny of files.

Start the program by typing its name, followed by an optional drive and file name in the usual format. The named file is the one that HEXDUMP will open and dump to the screen. If you omit the file name, HEXDUMP will ask you to enter it after it has started running. The program halts with a beep and an error message when the named file does not exist. Otherwise, it immediately dumps the first (Øth) block of the file.

At the top of each dumped block appears the name of the file and the currently displayed block number. The areas of the dump are identified by the headers "Offset" (the offset of the first byte of each 16-byte line within the current block), "Hex data," and "ASCII." In the ASCII field, alphanumerics and punctuation appear "as is," and all other bytes (lower than 32 or higher than 127) appear as periods.

At the bottom of the block, a menu asks you to choose what action you want to take next. This menu reads

**Q(uit), B(ackward), J(ump), any other key to continue...**

Type the indicated one-letter response for the desired action; it makes no difference if you type upper- or lowercase, and the response doesn't have to be followed by pressing ENTER.

"Q" immediately ends the program and returns you to DOS without clearing the screen. "B" takes you to the block preceding the current one (from block 9 to block 8, for instance). The "J" option allows you to jump around within the file at random, bypassing intervening blocks. When you type "J," a query appears below the menu line asking you to enter the 256-byte block number. The first block of the file (offset Ø–255) is block Ø, the bytes from 256–511 are block 1, etc. Thus, if you want to go 256Ø bytes into the file, the block number is 1Ø. You can use this selection to jump forward or backward. You cannot jump back beyond block Ø, and if you jump forward beyond the end of the file, the program tells you that you have reached the end of the data. Also, if end-of-file appears within a block, the program fills out the 16-byte line in which it occurs, and the next line advises you of end-of-file. Pressing any key other than "Q," "B," or "J" advances the dump to the next block in sequence (from block 5 to block 6, for example).

*Parameters:*   The name of the file to be dumped can optionally appear on the program command line.

*Functions Called:*   set_mode, set_page, clr_scrn, put_text, put_curs, clr_eos, upshift, txt_attr, dump16.

```
#include <stdio.h>

        /* HEXDUMP is a file-dump utility program */

    long     bof, block = 0L;     /* globals */
main ( argc, argv )
int      argc;
char     *argv [];
{
    char     fname [ 80 ], ta;
    int      fd;
    long     lseek();

        set_mode ( 2 );
        set-page ( 0 );
        clr_scrn ( 0 );
        ident();
        if ( argc == 1 ) {
            put_text ( 0, 5, 29, 0, "What is the filename?" );
            put_curs ( 0, 7, 32 );
            gets ( fname );
            put_curs ( 0, 4, 0 );
            clr_eos ( 0 );
        } else
            strcpy ( fname, argv [ 1 ] );
        upshift ( fname );
        if ( fd = fopen ( fname, "r" )) {
            bof = lseek ( fd, 0L, 2 );        /* end of file */
            dump ( fd, fname );
        } else {
            putchar ( 7 );                    /* beep */
            ta = txt_attr ( 0, 15, 1 );
            put_text ( 0, 8, 30, ta, "Sorry, no such file" );
        }
        put_curs ( 0, 22, 0 );
```

```c
}    /* -------------------------------------------------------- */
ident ()
{
    put_text ( 0, 0, 28, 0, "HEXDUMP UTILITY PROGRAM" );
    put_text ( 0, 1, 39, 0, "by" );
    put_text ( 0, 2, 35, 0, "Kent Porter" );
}    /* -------------------------------------------------------- */
dump ( fp, name )              /* dump the opened file */
int     fp;
char    name [];
{
    int     tmp [ 4 ], p, rc, addr;
    char    buff [ 16 ];
    long    cl, sk, ofst, lseek();
       put_curs ( 0, 1, 0 );
       bios ( 9, ´-´, 15, 79, 0, tmp );    /* cosmetic bar */
       put_curs ( 0, 2, 0 );
       clr_eos ( 0 );
       printf ( "\n%s", name );            /* identify dump */
       puts ( "\nOffset  Hex data" );
       put_curs ( 0, 4, 60 );
       puts ( "ASCII\n" );
       do {                                /* main dump loop */
           put_curs ( 0, 3, 50 );
           printf ( "Block %3LU", block ); /* 256-byte block */
           addr = 0;
           put_curs ( 0, 5, 0 );
           clr_eos ( 0 );
           ofst = block * 256L;
           ofst = ( ofst > bof ) ? bof : ofst; /* eof check */
           sk = lseek ( fp, ofst, 0 );
           for ( p = 0; p < 16; p++ ) {
               rc = read ( fp, buff, 16 );
               cl = ofst + ( long ) ( addr );  /* current loc */
               if ( cl < bof ) {
                   printf ( "%6d  ", addr );
                   dump16 ( buff );
                   addr += 16;
               } else {
                   puts ( "\n------------  END OF FILE" );
                   break;
               }
           }
       } while ( menu () != ´Q´ );
}    /* -------------------------------------------------------- */
int     menu ()
{
    char    choice;

        put_text ( 0, 22, 8, 0,
            "Q(uit), B(ack), J(ump), any other key to continue... " );
```

```
        switch ( choice = toupper ( getchar ())) {
            case 'B':   block = ( block > 0L ) ? block - 1 : 0L;
                        break;
            case 'J':   put_text ( 0, 23, 8, 0,
                            "256-byte block number? " );

                        scanf ( "%LU", &block );
                        block = ( block > 0L ) ? block : 0L;
                        break;
            default:    block += 1;
                        break;
        }
        return ( choice );
    }   /* -----------------------------------------------------------*/
```

## bar

## ( base, height, x, color )

*Description:*  This is a graphics function for IBM-type machines that is useful in constructing bar graphs. It draws a three-dimensional vertical bar that appears to be at the viewer's lower left (so that you see its front surface, top, and right side). It operates in screen modes 4 and 5 (320 × 200) and also in mode 6 (640 × 200).

The bottom of the bar rests on the vertical coordinate specified by base and its front surface height is given by the height parameter. The front surface is eight units wide. Because of the three-dimensional effect, the top slants to the right another four coordinate units and the right side adds four units to the overall width, so that the resulting bar is height + 4 units high and twelve units wide. The x parameter defines the horizontal position of the bar's left edge.

When operating in multicolor graphics (mode 5), the function outlines the bar in white and paints the front and top surfaces with the specified color. In other modes, the front and top are solid light unless you specify color Ø, in which case they are solid black.

With a little ingenuity, you can utilize this function to create very professional-looking graphs.

*Parameters:*

base is the vertical (normally but not necessarily in the range Ø–199, numbering downward) where the bottom of the bar rests.

height is the number of vertical units of height for the bar's front surface.

x is the horizontal coordinate (normally but not necessarily Ø–319 in modes 4 and 5, and Ø–639 in mode 6) of the left edge of the bar.

color is a valid color code for the current mode.

*Type of Value Returned:*  None.

*Other Functions Called:*  line, rd__mode.

```
bar ( base, height, x1, color )      /* 3-D bar for graph */
int   base, height, x1, color;
{
    int    x2, x3, y1, y2, y3, c, r [ 3 ];

        x2 = x1 + 7;
        x3 = x2 + 4;
        y1 = base - 4;
        y2 = base - height;
        y3 = y2 - 4;
        line ( x1, base, x2, y2, 3, 1 );
        line ( x3, y1, x1 + 4, y3, 3, 1 );
        line ( x1, y2, x1 + 4, y3, 3, 0 );
        line ( x2, y2, x3, y3, 3, 0 );
        line ( x2, base, x3, y1, 3, 0 );
        for ( c = x1 + 1; c < x2; c++ )
            line ( c, base - 1, c, y2 + 1, color, 0 );
        for ( c = x1 + 1; c <= x2; c++ )
            line ( c, y2 - 1, c + 3, y3 + 1, color, 0 );
        rd_mode ( r );
        if ( r [ 0 ] !_ 6 ) {
            y3 = height - 2;
            for ( c = x2 + 1, y2 = base - 2; c < x3; c++, y2-- )
                line ( c, y2, c, y2 - y3, 0, 0 );
        }
}
```

PLUME

# GET TO KNOW YOUR IBM® PC

(0452)

☐ **DOS PRIMER for the IBM® PC and XT**
**by Mitchell Waite, John Angermeyer, and Mark Noble.**
An easy-to-understand guide to IBM's disk operating-system, versions 1.1 and 2.0, which explains—from the ground up—what a DOS does and how to use it. Also covered are advanced topics such as the fixed disk, tree structured directories, and redirection.   (254949—$14.95)

☐ **PASCAL PRIMER for the IBM® PC**
**by Michael Pardee.**
An authoritative guide to this important structured language. Using sound and graphics examples, this book takes the reader from simple concepts to advanced topics such as files, linked lists, compilands, pointers, and the heap.   (254965—$17.95)

☐ **ASSEMBLY LANGUAGE PRIMER for the IBM® PC and XT**
**by Robert Lafore.**
This unusual book teaches assembly language to the beginner. The author's unique approach, using DEBUG and DOS functions, gets the reader programming fast without the usual confusion and overhead found in most books on this fundamental subject. Covers sound, graphics, and disk access.   (257115—$24.95)

☐ **BLUEBOOK OF ASSEMBLY ROUTINES for the IBM® PC and XT**
**by Christopher L. Morgan.**
A collection of expertly written "cookbook" routines that can be plugged in and used in any BASIC, Pascal, or assembly language program. Included are graphics, sound, and arithmetic conversions. Get the speed and power of assembly language in your program, even if you don't know the language!   (254981—$19.95)

---

All prices higher in Canada.

To order, use the convenient coupon on the next page.

Ⓟ
Computer Guides from PLUME